HASSLE-FREE
BOSTON

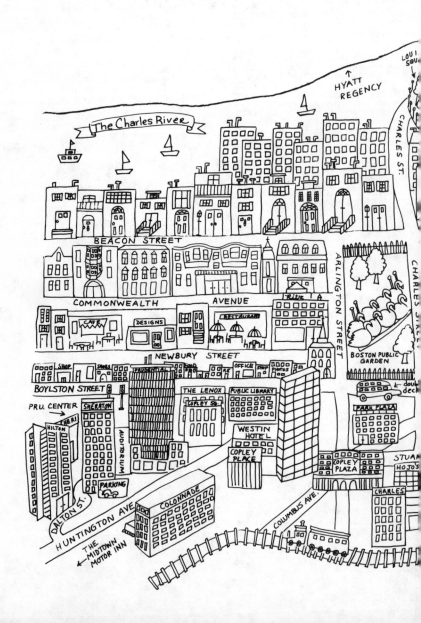

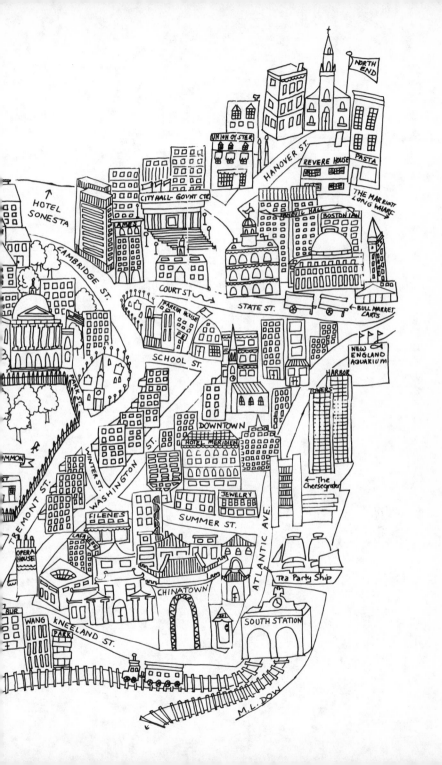

HASSLE-FREE BOSTON

A MANUAL FOR WOMEN

Mary Maynard
and
Mary-Lou Maynard Dow

The Lewis Publishing Company
Lexington, Massachusetts
Brattleboro, Vermont

Grateful Acknowledgment is made to those who supplied photographs for this book: page 1, courtesy of the Rhode Island Historical Society; page 42, James Scherer for WGBH; page 60, courtesy of *The Christian Science Monitor*; pages 62, 65, 71, 85, 91, 94, 119, 125, 128, 146, 149, 153, courtesy of Schlesinger Library, Radcliffe College; page 107, courtesy of Isabella Stewart Gardner Museum; page 115, courtesy of the Massachusetts State House Archives; page 134, courtesy of Louisa May Alcott Memorial Association; page 157, Paul J. Connell, *The Boston Globe;* page 161, courtesy of Wide World Photos, Inc.; pages 92 and 104, Ellen Shub.

Special acknowledgment to The Arthur and Elizabeth Schlesinger Library on the History of Women in America, the library at Radcliffe College that seeks to give the "other half of the story."

First Edition

Text copyright © 1984 by The Lewis Publishing Company

This book is manufactured in the United States of America. It is designed by Irving Perkins Associates and published by The Lewis Publishing Company, Fessenden Road, Brattleboro, Vermont 05301.

Distributed in the United States by E. P. Dutton, Inc., New York.

Library of Congress Cataloging in Publication Data

Maynard, Mary, 1929–
Hassle-free Boston.

Includes index.

1. Boston (Mass.)—Description—1981- —Guide-
books. 2 Women travelers—Massachusetts—Boston.
I. Dow, Mary-Lou Maynard, 1956- . II. Title.
F73.18.M39   1984   917.44'610443   84–809
ISBN 0–86616–040–X (pbk.)

For Pam and Holly, who helped,
and
for Jim, Jeff, and Andy, who applauded.

CONTENTS

FOREWORD

As the shallops ventured forth from the Mayflower and neared the
Plymouth shore on that cold, wintry November day in 1620, a young
woman standing in the bow of the lead boat eagerly jumped into the
chilly, shallow waters and waded ashore.

"I will be the first to step on that rock," she gallantly called over her
shoulder to the others. And thus the first Pilgrim to set foot on Plymouth Rock was a woman—Mary Chilton. She was also to be the first
woman and only Mayflower passenger who later "removed" permanently to Boston as one of the city's first residents.

History books, as we well know, do not properly document the vast
contributions that women have made to the development of any society; and Boston is no exception. Little is known, for instance, of the life
of Mary Chilton after she took that fateful leap. Only through arduous
research do we find that she had ten children, adopted another, and
was the ancestor of such distinguished Americans as John Copley,
Henry Wadsworth Longfellow, and the famous Boston Appletons.
Surely she must be considered a "founding mother" if nothing else.

Our goal in this guidebook, along with offering practical advice to the woman traveler and guest to this fair (poetically speaking) city, is to enlighten you as to the part that the indomitable and intelligent women who shaped our town have played.

Mary Chilton remains a symbol (the oldest and most exclusive women's club in town bears her name) of the spirit and vitality of the founding mothers — the sisters of liberty and daughters of the Revolution who truly made this city what it is today.

History books can only hint at the myriad hassles that the early women settlers such as Mary Chilton had to face in Boston. Lack of food, water, shelter, heat, sanitation, transportation, a few unfriendly Indians, and, in general, a hostile environment were but a few of her discomforts.

In slightly more than three hundred and fifty years most of these problems have been solved and, for the traveler who knows her way around, Boston can now be considered pretty much a hassle-free city.

This guidebook is intended to put you in touch with those services and accommodations best suited to women traveling alone, thus, it is to be hoped, eliminating needless frustrations. The selection of hotels and restaurants are not necessarily based on cost but on those establishments that offer the utmost in good value for women, i.e., service, safety, and convenience. Some hotels have not been included because they did not meet these requirements (except for those that will be opening after the date of publication). Some popular Boston restaurants have not been included because they failed the test of treating solo women customers on a par with single men.

Boston, like most large American cities, requires an alert and safety-conscious traveler. For instance, you don't stroll on Boston Common after dark, jog through the Arnold Arboretum without a partner, or use public transportation late at night. But officials, business establishments, proprietors, and concerned citizens are, for the most part, interested in your well-being as a guest to this city and are working toward making your visit a safe and happy one — or at best, hassle-free.

If you feel that any of the establishments listed here do not measure up, or if we have not included your favorite place, we would like to hear about it (P.O. Box 693, Weston, MA 02193) for possible inclusion in an updated version of this book.

DEBORAH SAMPSON GANNETT
1760-1827

Deborah Sampson Gannett, a.k.a. Robert Shurtliff, is the Official Heroine of the Commonwealth.

The Official Heroine of Massachusetts, Deborah Sampson Gannett, was a soldier in the Revolutionary War. The oldest of six children, she was a direct descendant of such good old Pilgrim forebears as Miles Standish and Priscilla and John Alden.

Her father deserted the family when Deborah was about ten years old. Because her mother had no means to support her children, Deborah was bound out as a servant to a family that kept a farm in Middleborough.

As a robust, healthy young girl (at five feet, eight inches she was very large for a girl at that time), she was soon handling most of the rugged farm chores as well as any of the men. When her term of service ended she set out on her own in search of adventure. Dressing in boys' clothes, she enlisted in the Continental army under the name of Robert Shurtliff. So clever was she at her disguise (and thanks to her above-average height, physical stamina, and strong features), that she concealed her identity for over eighteen months of service.

She took part in several military skirmishes. During one at Tarrytown, New York, she was shot in the thigh. She managed to dress her own wounds; but several months later, while defending the Capitol at Philadelphia, she fell victim to typhoid fever — and this time her true gender was discovered.

She was honorably discharged in 1783 at West Point, but without the usual soldier's pension. Several years later, married, and the mother of three children, she was aided by Paul Revere in securing not only a small pension but some back pay as well.

When she died in 1827, her husband (Benjamin Gannett), then ill himself, applied to the government for a widower's pension (the first such request). This time the Congress finally recognized Deborah as a fully accredited soldier and war hero and granted her husband *her* full pension.

In the summer of 1983, Deborah Sampson Gannett, a.k.a. Robert Shurtliff, was designated by the state House of Representatives as the Official Heroine of the Commonwealth.

1

GETTING ACQUAINTED WITH THE CITY

THE PROPER BOSTONIAN WARDROBE

There is a very good reason why Boston never has been and probably never will be the fashion capital of the world. It's simply a matter of our climate.

There's an old New England adage that says, "If you don't like the weather, just wait a minute." Mark Twain described it even more explicitly when he said, "I have counted 136 different kinds of weather here [in New England] inside twenty-four hours."

You can see that it's hard to be fashionable in open-toed shoes during an unexpected spring shower; in a sleeveless dress when the summer temperature suddenly plummets thirty degrees; or worse still, when the chilly autumn morning turns into a sizzling Indian-summer afternoon and you went off to work in a wool suit and knee-high leather boots.

Weather tables such as the one illustrated here are somewhat beneficial in helping you to determine just what to pack in your suitcase when

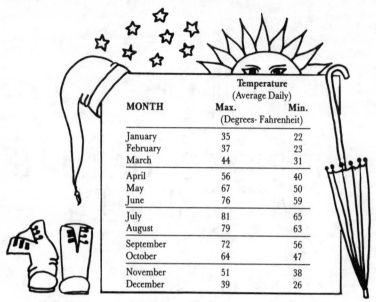

MONTH	Temperature (Average Daily)	
	Max.	Min.
	(Degrees- Fahrenheit)	
January	35	22
February	37	23
March	44	31
April	56	40
May	67	50
June	76	59
July	81	65
August	79	63
September	72	56
October	64	47
November	51	38
December	39	26

Boston's "mean" temperature

you're Boston-bound. But the following clarification is offered as a general rule of thumb.

It's reasonably safe to say that it is generally very cold in Boston from November through March. Along with the cold weather there is lots of snow and rain. It's not unheard of for Boston to get hit with a heavy snow storm even in April; the Easter Parade on the Common is often snowed on.

Therefore, wool clothes and other heavy fabrics are worn from October through April and lightweight materials thereafter. Boots are needed from November through March at least, and "sensible" shoes — ones good for walking on slippery bricks, in mud puddles, or on hot pavements — are *de rigueur* from April through October.

A current fad among Boston's downtown office workers is to wear running shoes to work and carry office shoes in a tote bag. (Jogging and walking are popular lunchtime activities in the city.)

The "layered look" was not a fashion trend here: It has been a way of life in Boston since Colonial women donned several sets of undergarments and three or four outer tops that could be peeled off as needed. The three-piece suit is worn all four seasons here and is the basic wardrobe to bring, along with assorted short- or long- sleeved blouses (depending on the season), and sweaters.

Unless you're going to a very special occasion you probably won't need anything spectacular. Ball gowns died out with the last waltz; and bangles and beads (called "creative dressing") are seen only at discos. The same outfit you put on in the morning will generally carry you through the evening (weather permitting) without breaking any fashion rules.

And a word of warning about "jeans": No matter what the cut, quality, label, or price tag, most Boston maitre d's still look upon jeans as barnyard attire. You will not be allowed to enter many of the better restaurants or bars if you are wearing them. Stories about Gloria Steinem, Jane Fonda, top fashion models, and other celebrities being turned away at the door of local establishments have become legends.

Conservative, practical, sensible, and thrifty are all words to describe the Boston wardrobe. Fashionable? If the alternative is chilblains, frostbite, hypothermia, or heat prostration, the answer is "yes!"

ACCOMMODATIONS

Like the city itself, Boston hotels represent a unique blending of past and present. While their ambiance and decor may reflect the early-American charm of Colonial Boston, their services and amenities range from the civilized to the utmost in contemporary luxury.

We have chosen the following hotels because they provide the best accommodations in the city for women travelers. Special features are pointed out in their individual descriptions.

In all of them security ranks high. Such details as assigning to women traveling alone the rooms nearest the elevators and on lower floors, twenty-four-hour guards checking corridors, escort service to your room at any hour of the night, and security-card lock systems are given serious attention.

At each of these hotels there is a concierge who is at your service to make dinner or theater reservations, employ a baby sitter, or set up just about anything you need. Valet services include cleaning, pressing, and mending your clothes; Housekeeping will supply you with such things as an iron, ironing board, blow-dryer, or curling iron. All these hotels have room service, most on a twenty-four-hour basis. Their basic policy is "ask and you shall receive"; it's just a matter of knowing what you can ask for.

Many times it's the small things that can make or break your trip. There's nothing worse than standing soaking wet in the shower and remembering that you left your shampoo at home. It's nice to know that these hotels have thought of all such essentials — from shampoo to skirt hangers.

In almost every hotel there is no charge for children under a certain age staying in their parents' room. The age limit varies in each hotel, though, so it is best to check first.

If you are planning to bring your pet you'll have to check into one of the following: Copley Plaza, Boston Park Plaza, Ritz, Holiday Inn, Parker House, Sheraton, Lenox, or Midtown.

We would recommend staying on the concierge floor if one is available at your hotel. It will cost a little more, but here you can attain the best in security and privacy as well as be treated with special attention. A private lounge on the floor will allow you to meet people in a less noisy and public environment; and, of course, it eliminates entertaining in your bedroom.

In most of the hotels listed here, the restaurants and cafes offer some of the finest dining in the city, thus saving you time and energy spent searching for a place to eat. Also, it's nice to know that Boston hotel maitre d's are well accustomed to women traveling solo and will not put you behind the potted palms.

Hotel lobby bars are, for the most part, friendly, hospitable spots where you can find some conversation or quietly sip and watch the "Hub" revolve.

Because hotel rates are constantly subject to change, we have used a fairly general rating system to give you an idea of prices. Based on single occupancy for one night we have classified the hotels as Luxury (over $100); Expensive ($70–$95); or Moderate ($50–$65).

MODERATE

The Copley Square Hotel

617-536-9000
toll-free res. 800-225-7062

47 Huntington Avenue $5 overnight parking; $2 each
Boston, MA 02116   time car is removed

One of Boston's oldest hotels, the Copley Square (in Back Bay) prides itself on serving families as well as being family-run itself. Women travelers with children will find the Family Suite facilities both economical and practical. Double bedrooms, each with TV and coffee maker, can be had with separate entranceways.

Pop's Patio, a pink-and-green indoor patio with umbrella tables, was named after "Pop," the owner, by his children. In direct contrast, the Cafe Budapest, a Hungarian restaurant complete with wandering violinists, is one of the most sophisticated dining spots in town. Upstairs, the Budapest Cafe Tearoom specializes in espresso and delicious pastries, while the Sports Saloon is all that its name implies. With its widescreen TV and casual atmosphere it is a gathering place for sports enthusiasts, particularly when the home team is on a winning streak — be it Red Sox, Celtics, Bruins, or Patriots.

Some of the best shopping — Saks, Lord & Taylor, and many boutiques — is close at hand; and Neiman-Marcus will soon be moving into the neighborhood.

The Lenox Hotel

710 Boylston Street
Boston, MA 02116

617-536-5300
toll-free res. 800-225-7676
$5 overnight parking; $2 each
time car is removed

The Lenox, another Boston landmark, is located in the heart of the Back Bay overlooking the Prudential Center and Copley Square. Shopping and sights are only steps away, and public transportation is at the door.

The rooms combine the charm of French, early-American, and Oriental furnishings. They offer coffee makers, AM-FM radios, and baskets filled with bath oil and shampoo; and some of the rooms contain original working fireplaces.

The Olde London Pub and Grille is reminiscent of sixteenth-century England and serves traditional New England fare, while Delmonico's serves gourmet cuisine in a Victorian-style setting. Diamond Jim's piano bar, where the sing-along is still alive, is a favorite after-theater spot with Bostonians.

A popular spot with business women as well, the Lenox was chosen by *Boston Magazine* in 1981 to host the magazine's designated 100 most powerful women in Boston. The celebration was attended by presidential-cabinet member Margaret Heckler, several women judges, and many outstanding women from the business community and the arts.

The Midtown Hotel

220 Huntington Avenue
Boston, MA 02115

617-262-1000
toll-free res. 800-242-1177
free parking

The two-story Midtown Hotel with its 160 rooms is popular with group travelers. Rates are on the inexpensive side and free parking — almost unheard of in the city — is a great advantage. Located across from the Christian Science center and the Prudential Center and a block from Symphony Hall, the Midtown offers great access for business or pleasure.

Spacious bedrooms have full-length mirrors and come in a variety of styles — with decor including frilly canopy beds, brass beds, or rattan furnishings. The Midtown prides itself on cleanliness. If you're the type to check under the bed, you'll find someone has already beaten you to it! The Executive Housekeeper leaves her card there with the message, "Hi, we have already looked under the bed to make certain it is clean and sanitary, thank you."

Breakfast, lunch, and dinner are served in the Colony Room; liquor, however, is not served on the premises. There are a beauty salon and a steam bath and massage, and during the summer guests can take a dip in the outdoor pool.

EXPENSIVE

Back Bay Hilton Hotel

Dalton & Belvidere Sts.
Boston, MA 02215

617-236-1100
toll-free res. 800-882-1653
$4 overnight parking

The Back Bay Hilton, located near the Prudential Center and Hynes Auditorium, offers bedroom views of the Charles River, the Back Bay, and the Christian Science complex. It is one of the newest hotels in Boston. Bedrooms are quite spacious, and there are two telephones in every room.

Extras include thick comfortable mattresses, full-length mirrors, sitting areas, brass and wood hangers and old sepia photos of Boston. Along with twenty-four-hour hotel security, there is also a security guard in the garage, cameras in every stairwell, and the Winfield Lock System on every door — which even keeps the maids out!

Women traveling with children will appreciate the Studio Apartment Suite with pull-out couch in the sitting area adjoining the bedroom. Murphy-bed-style rooms as well as facilities for the handicapped are available too. Corner rooms have balconies, and on each floor a door closes off the elevator area to lessen the noise.

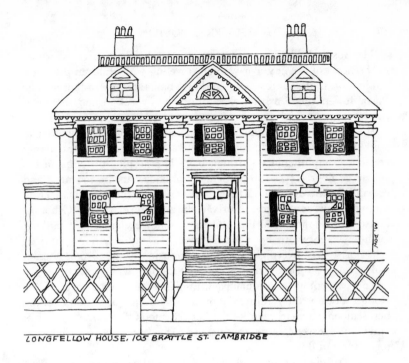

LONGFELLOW HOUSE, 105 BRATTLE ST. CAMBRIDGE

Special features of the Hilton are its gift shop, indoor swimming pool, and sun decks. Dalton's restaurant offers traditional American food in a casual atmosphere, and the adjoining Cafe (with ceiling fans and soda fountain) is a great stop for dessert or coffee. The Lobbyist Lounge, primarily frequented by hotel guests, is the perfect place to have your privacy and a cocktail too. But if you're in the mood for company, the Satin Doll Lounge on the lower level swings with big-band music and offers dancing nightly.

Boston Park Plaza Hotel & Towers

617-426-2000
toll-free res.
800-225-2008
free overnight valet parking; $1 each time car is
removed

50 Park Plaza
Boston, MA 02117

The Boston Park Plaza, minutes from the theater district, is located in the heart of the city. For women traveling with children there are family suites with double rooms and twin baths at no extra charge. The Plaza Towers offers private elevator, express check-in and check-out service, and concierge service to insure the best in security and privacy.

Special amenities in the Towers include newspapers delivered to your door, terrycloth bathrobe, private safe, refrigerator, skirt hangers, and complimentary garment bag. The hospitality room on the concierge floor serves complimentary breakfast in the morning and cocktails in the evening. Adjoining it is a small but elegant meeting room for short conferences or private dining at no extra cost. Other in-house features include airline offices, currency-exchange and banking facilities, twenty-four-hour room service, twenty-four-hour pharmacist, florist, free overnight parking, limousine to the airport, health club, beauty shop and massage, and gift shop.

You can enjoy traditional New England fare served in the Cafe Rouge, a restaurant reminiscent of the Victorian era, or at one of the best seafood places in town — the Legal Seafood Restaurant. The Fox and Hound serves continental cuisine and has been rated one of the top restaurants of Boston.

If you're planning a combination dinner/theater night, the Park Plaza offers complimentary limo service to the show. The Captain's Piano Bar, Plaza Pub, and Lobby Garden Lounge all offer entertainment and a place to relax after the show.

The Colonnade Hotel

	617-424-7000
120 Huntington Avenue	toll-free res. 800-323-7500
Boston, MA 02116	$4 overnight parking

The Colonnade, located in Back Bay, recently opened its doors to a newly renovated entrance and lobby. Luxurious rooms offer skirt hangers, assorted toiletries, and twenty-four-hour room service.

Other features include a hair salon, a sauna with body wrapping, facials, and a female masseuse for women only. In the summer you can enjoy the outdoor pool, cabanas, and putting green. On the first Friday of every month there is a fashion show sponsored by Saks Fifth Avenue in the Cafe Promenade.

The Colonnade is noted for its fine restaurants, notably the award-winning Zachary's. It's famous for its Friday afternoon buffet and distinctive wine list, not to mention its elegantly served continental food. The bar at Zachary's offers nightly jazz entertainment while piano music fills the lobby and tea-court restaurants. Zachary's takes everything seriously — including its dress code. Even Faye Dunaway was once asked to leave the bar because she was dressed — heaven forbid! — in blue jeans.

57 Park Plaza Hotel

(Howard Johnson's)	617-482-1800
200 Stuart Street	toll-free res. 800-654-2000
Boston, MA 02116	free overnight parking

The 57 Park Plaza, adjacent to the theater district, offers a variety of inexpensive accommodations for the traveling executive. Every bedroom has its own private balcony large enough for a small party of people. Full-length mirrors enhance the contemporary decor. The Executive single room and Executive mini-suite both come with double bed and sitting room, and both are reasonably priced.

Other services include a heated indoor pool, sauna and sun deck, HBO, and a hair salon; and racquetball court time can be arranged at a nearby facility. A Howard Johnson's restaurant is on the premises; and the 57 Restaurant, with its dazzling central fountain and Oriental decor, offers seafood and prime ribs. The 57 Lounge has nightly entertainment and dancing.

The Sheraton-Boston Hotel

Prudential Center	617-236-2000
39 Dalton Street	toll-free res. 800-325-3535
Boston, MA 02199	$5.50 overnight parking

The Sheraton Boston, located in the convenient Prudential Center, is the largest hotel in New England. Bedrooms and baths are stocked with shampoos, soaps, and skirt and padded hangers. There is twenty-four-hour room service, as well as a five-minute breakfast service with rolls and coffee. The indoor-outdoor pool with retractable glass roof is reminiscent of the tropics with "lanai" bedrooms around the pool and Jacuzzi.

Auto-rental and airline offices are on the premises and special floors are designated for flight attendants and business people. For the traveling single woman, the Captain's Table offers a chance to dine with others.

The Sheraton Towers has private check-in, private elevators, and a security card locking system on each door to insure the ultimate in safety. Rooms come with makeup mirrors, fresh flowers and mints, deluxe towels, baskets filled with lotions and hair care items, newspapers, in-house movies, and telephones in the bathrooms. The private lounge, overlooking the Boston skyline, offers continental breakfast in the morning and complimentary hors d'oeuvres at cocktail hour.

The Sheraton's fine restaurants include the four-star Apley's, serving American food; the Kon Tiki for Szechuan and Cantonese cuisine; and the Mass. Bay Seacoast Co., serving, among other things, its award-winning clam chowder. "Lobsters to go" make the perfect New England gift and, given notice, the restaurant will pack them to travel.

The Sheraton goes all out for the women in the Boston Marathon, as this is the hotel that most of them choose to stay at.

Hotel Sonesta

	617-491-3600
5 Cambridge Parkway	toll-free res. 800-343-7170
Cambridge, MA 02142	free parking

The Hotel Sonesta is expanding its original building and plans to be completed in June of 1984. It is three miles from Logan Airport and is situated on the Charles River, which allows each room to have a fantastic view.

Currently the rooms are tastefully decorated with brick walls and floral patterns, while makeup mirrors and baskets of soaps and shampoo enhance the bathrooms. The turn-down service leaves a mint on your pillow. (The new guest rooms will also offer digital clocks, pulsating shower heads, and oversized towels.)

Other features include complimentary van service to the Marketplace and major businesses around Boston and Cambridge, one-day valet service, pool and health center, and a bell staff. (The new addition will have a full concierge service.)

Security at the Sonesta means twenty-four-hour guards patrolling the outdoor parking lot and hotel corridors. The main doors are locked at 11:00 p.m.

The Greenhouse Restaurant serves all meals and is a favorite lunch spot with local female executives. The Rib Room is a bit more formal, with oak walls and leather seats; it serves continental cuisine. A harpist plays in the Haypenny Lounge, and off the lobby at the Charles Bar is a piano bar.

Hyatt Regency Cambridge

	617-492-1234
575 Memorial Drive	toll-free res. 800-228-9000
Cambridge, MA 02139	$5 overnight parking

The Hyatt Regency, an architectural wonder, is located on the banks of the Charles River. Its shape is a ziggurat — to give every room the maximum view of the Boston skyline — and its lobby is filled with trees and fountains. And what would a Hyatt Regency be without its spectacular centrally located glass elevator that climbs to the ceiling?

The bedrooms, some with terraces overlooking the Charles, offer in-house movies and complimentary shoe-shine service. If you are a woman traveling alone you'll be given a welcome call once you've settled in; and dining arrangements will be made if you care to sit with others in the restaurant.

Each room on the Regency Club floor features a free newspaper, a wicker basket filled with toiletries, bathrobe, clock radio, flowers and chocolates, personalized matches, and Perrier water. The hospitality room offers continental breakfast in the morning and complimentary drinks and hors d'oeuvres from 5:00 to 7:00 p.m. Cordials are served from 7:00 to 11:00 p.m.

There are two gift shops and a jewelry store in the lobby.

The Empress restaurant serves continental food as well as Szechuan and Mandarin dishes. Jonah's, an indoor terrace overlooking the atrium, serves New England seafood and Italian and American cuisine. An oyster bar is also located here. The Pallysadoe, a parklike lounge, has entertainment six nights a week; and the Spinnaker Lounge, a popular meeting place, revolves slowly and affords a constantly changing panoramic view of Boston and Cambridge.

Logan Airport Hilton

Logan International Airport
East Boston, MA 02128

617-569-9300
toll-free res. 800-882-1653
free parking

The Logan Hilton is the only hotel inside Logan International Airport, and its primary purpose is to serve the air-traveling public. In fact, 80 percent of its guests stay for only one night.

Women traveling alone are given rooms in the main tower, which is closest to the lobby. Amenities include skirt hangers, clotheslines, sewing kits, triple-lock doors, and in-room movies. You can be assured of a good night's sleep because the hotel has been so constructed that planes cannot be heard landing or taking off at the airport.

Other services offered are currency exchange, free parking, free twenty-four-hour shuttle service to all airlines, outdoor pool, daily aerobics classes, and a gift shop in the lobby.

Appleton's Saloon features steak and fresh seafood as well as its good clam chowder; and the Glass Garden coffee shop serves light meals and cocktails from 6:30 a.m. until midnight. Both restaurants, by the way, have menus in braille.

The Inn at Children's

342 Longwood Avenue	617-731-4700
Boston, MA 02115	$2 overnight parking

The name of this gracious little hotel is rather misleading, because it is not just for children; nor is it just for those connected with Children's Hospital. It is, however, located in the heart of a great cluster of hospitals. So anyone having business at any of these hospitals would do well to reserve here.

The eighty-two nicely decorated rooms (several junior suites) come with TV, in-room movies, and room service until 11:00 p.m. There are an outdoor pool (in season), several small retail stores, banks, and pharmacies close by. The staff here is bilingual; and in the two restaurants (Sterling's for dinner and The Cafe for casual dining) the menu is available in Spanish. There is dancing in the bar from happy hour until closing.

While this hotel is quite a way out from the center of town, the MBTA Green Line is close at hand. The hotel has twenty-four-hour security, as do most of the buildings surrounding it; but it is not considered a safe neighborhood to walk around in after dark. If you are going to be out late it is best to take a taxi directly to your hotel.

LUXURY

The Copley Plaza

	617-267-5300
138 St. James Avenue	toll-free res. 800-225-7654
Boston, MA 02116	$6 overnight parking

The Copley Plaza (Back Bay) is considered the grande dame of Boston hotels. Elegant rooms have brass beds, full-length mirrors, and large closets; special soaps and creams are neatly packaged in each bathroom.

English Tea with finger sandwiches is served from 3:00 to 5:00 p.m. in proper Bostonian style. The Cafe Plaza offers continental dining, and traditional New England fare in the grand manner is served in

Copley's restaurant. The Plaza Bar and Library Bar are both excellent places to unwind.

Perfume and jewelry shops as well as Christaldi's hair salon are located just off the lobby. And only the Plaza would think to have on hand at the front desk a survival kit which includes paper pajamas, a nip of bourbon, a dime to call home, and a few other necessities, for those who may get stranded.

The Copley is a favorite with working women and royalty alike. King Saud of Saudi Arabia recently stayed there with two of his wives. Only female employees were allowed to serve the wives, who had to settle for room service as they were not allowed (by custom) to have dinner in the Grand Ballroom with the rest of the entourage.

The Ritz-Carlton Hotel

15 Arlington Street
Boston, MA 02117

617-536-5700
toll-free res. 800-992-8000
$10 overnight parking

The Ritz-Carlton offers traditional gracious living. Its unpretentious yet luxurious accommodations are the epitome of the "proper Bostonian" style. Many of the rooms overlook the Public Garden, and most bedrooms have fireplaces with a fresh supply of Vermont wood provided on a wintry day. Each bathroom is stocked with potpourri, Evelyn Crabtree bath cubes and shampoo, a sewing kit, and a clothesline.

The Ritz provides the ultimate in security. Room numbers are never given out or announced in the lobby. Separate keys lock your bedroom closets, and the main door is locked at 1:00 a.m.; entrance phones call the doorman. Each room has a call button for twenty-four-hour room service, and there are pantries on each floor for quick delivery. The Night Butler is ready to handle all requests at any hour of the evening. An attendant is designated to every other floor for special attention.

Elevator operators — with white gloves — are still in attendance. The Ritz is not a convention hotel but caters to singles and small groups, thus insuring privacy and quiet.

There are a hair salon and manicurist, drug and jewelry stores, a dress shop, a florist, and a podiatrist. The Ritz dining room serves continental cuisine. For less formal meals the Cafe, with windows overlooking Newbury Street, is a favorite spot. The Ritz Bar is a legend in itself; and the second-floor lounge for lunch, drinks, or snacks offers an unhurried sanctuary for finishing up paperwork or just relaxing with friends.

The Ritz is absolutely unbending when it comes to its dress code — jackets and ties for gentlemen and skirts for ladies. The only woman we ever heard of who cracked that code was Gloria Steinem.

The Hotel Meridien

	617-451-1900
250 Franklin Street	toll-free res. 800-223-9918
Boston, MA 02110	$12 valet parking

The Hotel Meridien is one of the newer hotels in Boston and is located in what many Bostonians will continue to refer to as "the old Federal Reserve Bank of Boston." Located in the heart of the financial district, yet minutes away from the Marketplace, sightseeing, and shopping, the hotel is another example of blending the new with the best of the old. The hotel has an international flair, with bedrooms designed in Oriental motifs. All have excellent views, sitting areas, and plants; and each employs the security card lock system that can be reprogrammed in minutes in case of loss or damage.

The rooms are nicely appointed with European scales, sewing kits, soaps and shampoos, full-length mirrors, and phones in the bathrooms. A special feature is the in-room mini-bar with nips of liquor and mixers. Twenty-four-hour room service (which includes the daily newspaper) is offered as well. In the evening, the turn-down service includes fresh mints on your pillow and a weather report left at your bedside.

Off the lobby you'll find a pharmacy, jewelry store, and florist. Fancies, a boutique selling perfumes, candies, wool blankets, and other attractive items, will do corporate gifting.

The restaurants in the hotel have an international flavor. There are damask linens, imported china, and wing-backed chairs. The Julien Lounge is warm and inviting, with plush sofas and a mahogany bar; it is a comfortable spot for visiting with friends. The Cafe Fleuri, a six-story atrium, serves American dishes, has an oyster bar, and serves Sunday brunch.

The Westin Hotel

Copley Place	617-262-9600
10 Huntington Avenue	toll-free res. 800-228-3000
Boston, MA 02117	$10 overnight parking

The Westin is one of Boston's newest hotels and is located in the also new Copley Place — a large, modern complex of hotels, restaurants, specialty stores, and theatres in the Back Bay area.

The focal point of the Westin's dramatic front entrance on Huntington Avenue is a large waterfall surrounding the up and down escalators. The furnishings of the hotel blend contemporary and traditional styles.

This convention-oriented hotel has many features catering to the handicapped person. Two separate floors encompassing forty rooms have been equipped to handle special problems. Elevator bells signal the floor level for the sight-impaired, and a lift has been installed in the year-round pool to assist the disabled.

The rooms are nicely appointed with comfortable furnishings and remote-control TV (sometimes hidden in armoires). Each bathroom is stocked with shampoo, toothpaste, and extra soap as well as a clothesline. Many of these rooms have views of the Charles River and Boston Harbor. Twenty-four-hour room service is available too.

The lobby lounge on the second floor is large and definitely a place for scheduling a relaxing business appointment. (High Tea and string quartets in the late afternoon.)

There are three restaurants, each with its own specialty. The Brasserie offers moderately priced casual dining; Turner Fisheries Bar and restaurant New England fresh seafood; and Ten Huntington a more elegant and varied dinner menu.

Several shops are located within the hotel — Discoveries (sundries, periodicals, gourmet food, liquors, and gifts); Mark Cross (leather goods); Ciro Jewelers; and Plantae (some of the most exotic floral arrangements ever seen in Boston).

The Skybridge, a walkway to the rest of Copley Place, will take you to Neiman-Marcus as well as other specialty shops and nine Sack movie theaters.

The Parker House Hotel

	617-227-8600
60 School Street	toll-free res. 800-228-2121
Boston, MA 02107	$11 overnight valet parking

The Parker House is the oldest continuously operated hotel in America, having kept its doors open on the same site since 1855. It is also the "Official Freedom Trail Hotel," located directly on the trail, and steeped in history itself. Rooms have been recently refurbished in contemporary motifs, and all are well appointed.

Women travelers are given the rooms closest to the elevators, rooms which come equipped with skirt hangers, full-length mirrors, solid marble bathrooms, Vidal Sassoon shampoo, and soaps from Ireland. Complimentary shoe shine, HBO, and twenty-four-hour room service are provided. Mini-suites offer spacious accommodations with parlors, plants, and dressing rooms.

Repeat guests become "VIP" and receive a gift from the General Manager's office on each subsequent stay. The ESP (Executive Service Plan) is worth checking into — a free membership offers extra amenities at no cost. There are gift, jewelry, and florist shops just off the lobby; limo service to the airport; and a special feature for joggers — complimentary orange juice and maps in the morning!

The hotel's formal dining room, Parker's, which has been rated by many as the finest in Boston, serves nouvelle cuisine in an elegant atmosphere. The popular Last Hurrah serves beef and seafood selections in a lively turn-of-the-century saloon. Bo Winiker's swing band performs here nightly and during Sunday brunch. The Cafe Tremont is a European-style cafe on the main floor offering nouvelle cuisine, an evening wine bar, and a take-home dessert counter. The Parker's Bar with piano music and the Lobby Bar are as popular with people who live or work in the neighborhood as with hotel guests.

The Parker House, with its special low-rate single room, has been a favorite with women travelers for generations. Author Willa Cather liked it so much she stayed for a whole year. And when the annual meetings of the American Suffrage Association were held in Boston in the late 1800s, the women delegates all stayed at the Parker House.

The Bostonian Hotel

Faneuil Hall Marketplace
Boston, MA 02109

617-523-3600
toll-free res. 800-343-0922
$15 overnight valet parking

The Bostonian Hotel is located just opposite the famous Quincy Market. This alone gives hotel guests great access to some of the finest shops in Boston, as well as fascinating views from their rooms. Most of the bedrooms feature floor-to-ceiling French windows, iron-railed balconies, Jacuzzi-styled tubs, and phones in the bathrooms. Most of the rooms in the Harkness Wing have exposed beams, brick walls, and working fireplaces.

Its WTA (Women Traveling Alone) rooms are placed close to elevators and have no connecting doors; and the amenities include Woolite and skirt hangers in the bathrooms. Other services available in the hotel include a hair salon offering facials and massage and private check-in with a designated host.

The decor is contemporary elegance tempered by traditional Beacon Hill charm. The glass-enclosed elevator will deliver you to the Seasons restaurant (the menus change four times each year) where classic New England fare is served. To end — or begin — your day, the Lobby Bar provides piano music at night and the Atrium Cafe serves complimentary coffee in the morning.

Boston Marriott Hotel

Long Wharf	617-227-0800
296 State Street	toll-free res. 800-228-9290
Boston, MA 02116	$10 valet parking

Located at historic Long Wharf and seconds away from Faneuil Hall Marketplace, the Boston Marriott offers modern conveniences in an unusual setting. Guests enter the lobby of the now famous red pyramid by way of an escalator located right at the front door. All of the 370 rooms offer interesting views of the marketplace. The Concierge Floor has a lounge serving complimentary breakfast in the morning and a cocktail bar at night. The rooms are well supplied with deluxe towels, shoe shine, perfume, and telephones in the bathroom.

Other features include a game room and indoor pool, sun deck, sauna, exercise room, and hydrotherapy pool. Also, a laundry room is supplied for those who would rather wash their own clothing. The gift shop sells men's and women's clothing as well as a good selection of New England gifts.

The Harbor Terrace Restaurant serves nouvelle cuisine while the Palm Garden offers family-style dining. At Rachael's Lounge, you can dance and sip cocktails while overlooking the Boston skyline. (The Boston Marriott Hotel at Copley Place will open in the spring of 1984.)

Hotel Intercontinental

One Boston Place	
Boston, MA 02108	617-451-2600

This twenty-two-story, 500-room hotel will be situated within the new Lafayette Place, a $130-million mixed-use complex in downtown Boston. Lafayette Place will offer 187 retail stores, twenty-three restaurants and cafes, and parking facilities; therefore, guests at the hotel will have every convenience nearby. The hotel itself will feature a restaurant and pub, swimming pool, sun terrace, and health club. Its decor is described as "a modern, cosmopolitan design concept, Jeffersonian in influence."

OTHER HOTELS IN THE BOSTON AREA

Holiday Inn
  Government Center   617-742-7630
  5 Blossom Street   toll-free res. 800-238-8000
  Boston, MA 02114

Howard Johnson's Motor Lodge/Fenway
  1271 Boylston Street   617-267-8300
  Boston, MA 02215   toll-free res. 800-654-2000

Howard Johnson's
  Kenmore Square   617-267-3100
  575 Commonwealth Avenue   toll-free res.
  Boston, MA 02215   800-654-2000

Howard Johnson's Motor Lodge
  Southeast Expressway, Exit 16   617-288-3030
  Andrew Square, Dorchester   toll-free res.
  Boston, MA 02125   800-654-2000

Ramada Inn-Boston Airport
  228 McClellan Highway   617-569-5250
  East Boston, MA 02128   toll-free res. 800-228-2828

Holiday Inn
  1651 Massachusetts Avenue   617-491-1000
  Cambridge, MA 02138   toll-free res. 800-238-8000

Howard Johnson's Motor Lodge
  777 Memorial Drive   617-492-7777
  Cambridge, MA 02139   toll-free res. 800-654-2000

Sheraton Commander Hotel
  16 Garden Street   617-547-4800
  Cambridge, MA 02138   toll-free res. 800-325-3535

FOR WOMEN ONLY

Berkeley Residence Club (YWCA)
  40 Berkeley Street   617-482-8850
  Boston, MA 02116 $2 YWCA membership
                           required

The Berkeley is located in the South End of Boston — an area that has been going through extensive revitalization. The Club has the atmosphere of a well-run college dormitory, with many of the guests sharing bathroom facilities. The bedrooms are clean and modestly furnished, and the reception rooms, lounge area, and game rooms are comfortable and cozy.

There are a limited number of rooms with sinks and private baths, but it is wise to call ahead to reserve one if this is your preference.

Cambridge YWCA

7 Temple Street   617-491-6050
Cambridge, MA 02139 $2 YWCA membership
                                       required

The Cambridge Y is mainly a residential facility for members only, but it has several single rooms available for tourists. The maximum stay is one week. Guests have access to the pool and sports facilities for a small additional fee. There are a TV lounge and community kitchen and laundry facilities. The staff is multilingual.

The Women's City Club of Boston

40 Beacon Street
Boston, MA 02108   617-227-3550

The Women's City Club is located in one of the fine old Beacon Hill houses. The house was built by Nathan Appleton in 1816, and in 1843 his daughter Fanny was married in the front parlor to Henry Wadsworth Longfellow. The Women's City Club, which was organized in 1913, moved into the building in 1916. The purpose of the Club, founded by several prominent Boston women, was to "promote the welfare of the city"; and it was very popular up until the 1950s. Recently the Club embarked on an ambitious development project to attract Boston's expanding population of professional women.

At present, the Club has twenty-six overnight rooms ranging from large, elegant rooms with private baths overlooking the Boston Common, to smaller rooms sharing baths. This is a private club — for members and their guests only — so arrangements must be made in advance. Reciprocal privileges are extended to members of other women's city clubs.

Luncheon is served daily; also Sunday brunch and Wednesday evening dinner. There are quiet work areas, informal conversation areas, a game room, and a small library. Plans are under way to add athletic facilities in the near future.

SOMETHING DIFFERENT

The Business Townhouse
   70–10 Kirkland Street
   Cambridge, MA 02138   617-868-2873

This furnished one-bedroom, four-level townhouse is enhanced with Mexican tile and oak floors, skylights, ceiling fans, wood stoves and plants. Included are kitchen, living room, and washer/dryer; several units available, three-day minimum, $100 per night, car available.

Stoneholm Street Apartments
   12 Stoneholm Street (Back Bay)   617-536-3506
   Boston, MA 02115   617-247-9844

Short- or long-term apartments near Prudential Center.

New Boston Properties, Inc.
   53 Hereford Street   617-262-3354
   Boston, MA 02115   617-262-3355

Run by two women who have over 250 newly remodeled, nicely furnished studios and one- and two-bedroom apartments in Back Bay and Beacon Hill. All are supplied with linens and kitchenware, and some have saunas and Jacuzzis. There is a one-week minimum stay.

Home Away
   66 Mt. Vernon Street
   Boston, MA 02108   617-523-1432

Short-term furnished apartments in Back Bay and Beacon Hill.

BED AND BREAKFAST

Bed & Breakfast Associates Bay Colony Ltd.
   P.O. Box 166
   Babson Park Branch
   Boston, MA 02157   617-872-6990

A reservation service to locate comfortable room and board in the warmth of private homes or inns in Boston and its suburbs.

New England Bed & Breakfast
1045 Centre Street
Newton, MA 02159   617-498-9819

Clean, comfortable rooms in Boston and suburbs. All within walking distance of public transportation. No minimum stay.

City Cousins Inc.
111 Lakeview Ave.
Cambridge, MA 02138   617-369-8416

A bed-and-breakfast reservation service with a variety of accommodations in greater Boston and the North Shore. Owned by three professional women, it specializes in serving the professional visitor who
has particular interests.

RELOCATING

Finding an affordable, safe, convenient, and livable apartment in
any large city is never an easy job. And when you add to that the com-
plication of a city like Boston, seemingly devoid of any comprehensive
geographical plan, it becomes a mind-boggling task.

You will soon discover that much of downtown Boston is, quite literally, laid out along the legendary cow paths; and any attempt to find
order among the maze of one way, dead-end, and blind-alley streets is
almost an impossibility. New buildings spring up in the middle of exist-
ing streets, while old street names fluctuate at the whim of new politicians — constantly rendering guides and maps obsolete.

Unless you are already familiar with Boston's eccentricities or can
depend on friends and coworkers to help with your search for a place to
live, it's best to take the time to study the city before putting down the
necessary two months' (in most cases) deposit or signing a lease (almost
always required).

You may want to take advantage of temporary housing facilities
such as those listed on page 20 while scouting around. The Berkeley
Residence for Women, for example, provides economical accommodations on a daily, weekly, or monthly basis and has many conveniences
— including meals.

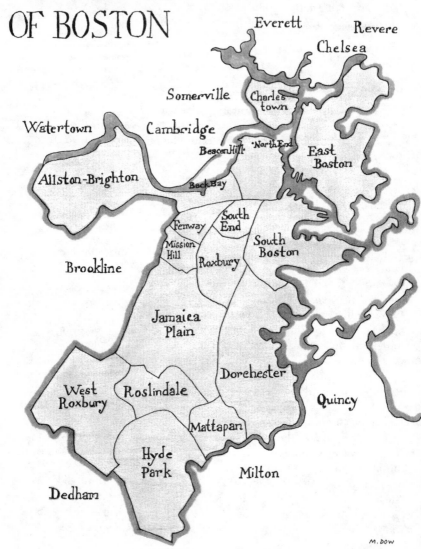

NEIGHBORHOODS
OF BOSTON

Everett

Revere

Chelsea

Somerville

Charles town

Watertown

Cambridge

North End

East Boston

Beacon Hill

Allston-Brighton

Back Bay

Fenway

South End

Mission Hill

South Boston

Brookline

Roxbury

Jamaica Plain

Dorchester

West Roxbury

Roslindale

Quincy

Mattapan

Hyde Park

Milton

Dedham

M. DOW

Getting to and from work will naturally put location high on your priority list, so a few basic facts about transportation are in order. Public transportation, the Massachusetts Bay Transit Authority (MBTA), more commonly called the T, consists of buses, subway trains, and trolley buses, and is reasonably inexpensive and usually reliable. Everyone who works in downtown Boston or the environs depends on it sooner or later; consequently you'll want to know it well (see page 34 for more details).

Buses and trains run regularly to many suburbs, so the possibility of finding a suitable apartment outside the city limits but within easy commuting distance should certainly be considered.

Every neighborhood or suburb has a distinct personality with certain advantages and disadvantages; therefore, it's just a matter of deciding what your own particular needs and lifestyle are — and what you can afford. The more desirable a neighborhood, naturally, the more expensive the accommodations will be. You will quickly learn, for instance, that Brookline is more expensive than Brighton even though the two towns seem to blend into one another.

We have listed below many of Boston's neighborhoods and surrounding towns with brief profiles, approximate rent prices, and accessibility to public transportation.

Aside from finding the right location, you should arm yourself with some important legal facts. The Massachusetts Consumer's Council (MCC) has put out a handy little booklet (available free at the State House Bookstore), which explains all landlord-tenant transactions. It's called *Shopping for an Apartment* and it will fill you in on such details as security deposits, sanitary codes, discrimination, misrepresentation, and how to deal with such.

It will also give you some of the important points to consider regarding the selection of a rental agent. If you decide to go it alone, there are hints as to what you should be wary of in false real-estate advertising — i.e., "blind," "bait-and-switch," and discriminatory ads. While all of these practices are illegal, they unfortunately still go on.

The last page of the booklet gives you a good checklist to take along while inspecting an apartment and lists some of the important questions to ask the landlord. For instance, when you see the trash barrels in the back hall, don't forget to ask who collects the garbage and how often, and who pays.

If you decide on the do-it-yourself route, the *Boston Sunday Globe* Real Estate section offers the widest selection of rentals — from the basement apartment to the penthouse. However, if you choose to look for something in the suburbs, you may want to try local community papers. Most of them are weeklies and can be picked up at neighborhood drugstores.

Aside from the older two- or three-family houses, there are now many apartment communities being developed in the suburbs. While it will take you longer to get to work, they do offer many amenities that may make the long commute worthwhile. Such things as swimming pools, athletic facilities, day-care services, laundries, and a variety of social activities are offered.

Other Real Estate sections to check out are those of the *Phoenix, The Tab*, and *Sojourner*. These papers have long columns of ads from people who are looking for roommates to share apartments and houses with. There are many practical and economical advantages of going this route. It saves you the expense of preliminary fees (utility deposits, telephone installation, etc.), and, of course, it gives you an opportunity to widen your circle of friends.

If you are to be affiliated with one of the universities and plan to live in an area such as Harvard Square, Kendall Square, or Kenmore Square, there are student/faculty housing offices with listings, as well as college newspapers, and myriad bulletin boards in these locations to look at.

Security and safety should also be high on your priority list when you shop for an apartment, and should never be sacrificed. Not everyone can afford to move into a building with a twenty-four-hour concierge, so there are some essential things to check on to make sure your building is just as safe.

Front doors should be kept locked at all times, with only residents owning keys. If your apartment is on other than the first floor, check to see if there is an intercom system so that you won't be running up and down stairs unnecessarily. You may want to install your own apartment door lock to insure safety, or at least inquire about having this done.

The entranceway and all corridors should be well lighted; and if you are on the ground floor, make sure all window locks are intact. Check all of these things while you are inspecting the apartment; and if anything is in need of repair, make sure that the work is done before you sign the lease. Where your safety is concerned, don't rely on promises.

Before you decide on your location, be sure to check out the convenience of such things as grocery stores, laundry facilities, and public transportation. If you own a car, there are several other things to look for: availability of parking, winter storm regulations, street-cleaning procedures, and residents' stickers. Parking restrictions are strictly enforced in the city — and the "Denver boot" is notorious.

Be sure to take note of the area surrounding the "T" stop or bus station you will be using regularly. Make sure it is located in a well-lighted, well-used area. Deserted "T" stops should definitely be avoided after dark.

If you aspire to such luxurious digs as the recently opened Devonshire Apartments — complete with twenty-four-hour concierge, athletic facilities, and multiple services, and located in the heart of the financial district — but can't afford it just yet, don't despair. We heard that among their well-heeled tenants (CEOs, presidents, board members, etc.), many are women.

THE NEIGHBORHOODS

Back Bay   One of the most desirable and expensive areas in the city. It encompasses the broad tree-lined boulevard of Commonwealth Avenue, Newbury Street and the Pru for shopping, and Beacon Street running along the Charles River with the best river views in town. It's difficult to find a one-bedroom apartment here for under $400, and for two bedrooms you can expect to pay anywhere from $600 to $3000 a month. Many of the old townhouses and apartment buildings are now being converted into condominiums, and one-bedroom condos start at $60,000 and up. Several real-estate firms handling this area can be found on Newbury Street. (MBTA Green Line.)

Beacon Hill   A small, sophisticated village in the heart of the city, and the oldest continuing residential part of Boston. Trendy shops, gourmet restaurants, and the possibility of being within walking distance of work (if you work downtown) make this neighborhood tops on apartment-seekers' lists. Check the outdoor bulletin boards (or windows) of the many real-estate offices along Charles Street. Studios start at $350 and one-bedroom apartments at $425. All MBTA lines connect at Park Street station on the Boston Common, which is close by.

Brighton-Allston   Students and young working people are attracted to this area by its affordable rents and close promixity to the uni-

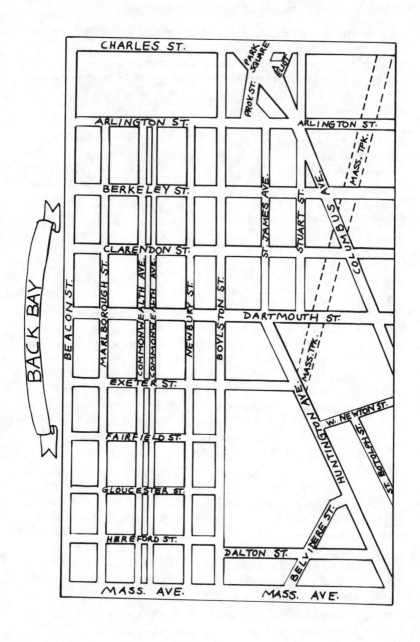

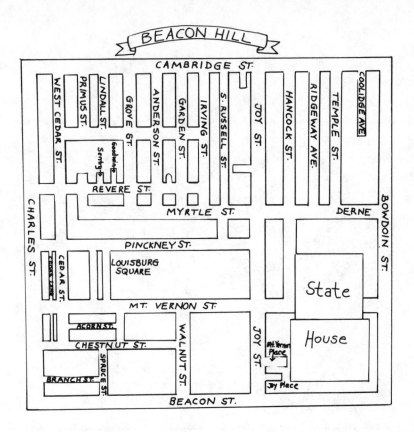

versies (Harvard, MIT, BU, Northeastern, BC, etc.). Also there is excellent transportation available via the MBTA Green Line and buses. An average two-bedroom apartment rents for $500 a month, and there are also a lot of opportunities for finding roommates and sharing here.

Charlestown Steeped in history and older than Beacon Hill, this area has recently seen tremendous changes through urban renewal. Many of the older homes have been restored and old buildings converted to new apartments. If you're lucky you might rent a two-bedroom apartment for $500 with a view of Old Ironsides or the Bunker Hill Monument thrown in. Only a few minutes from downtown Boston on the MBTA Orange Line and frequent bus service.

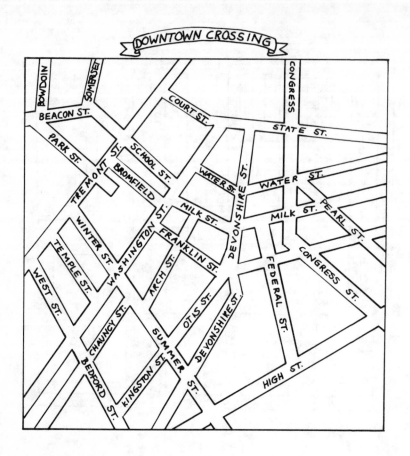

Dorchester A multiethnic neighborhood with many triple-deckers, apartments, and single- and two-family houses, as well as many small business establishments. Rents are more reasonable here than elsewhere in the city, but security is minimal in some areas. Two-bedroom apartments begin at $370, and the commuting to Boston is fast — via the MBTA Red Line with trolley connections and frequent bus service.

East Boston Dominated by Logan International Airport and the home of Suffolk Downs racetrack, this predominantly Italian neighborhood consists of row houses, triple- and double-deckers, and single-family homes. A two-bedroom apartment can be found for under $400 here, but if you drive a car and have to use the tunnel every day, it may not be worth it. Otherwise, the MBTA Blue Line provides quick access to downtown Boston.

Hyde Park   This is the farthest outlying part of the city, with mostly one-family homes giving it a suburban atmosphere. Distance from the center of things keeps the rents minimal — $325 for a two-bedroom apartment — but transportation can be a problem. There are trains on weekdays that connect to Back Bay and South Station as well as buses to the MBTA Orange Line.

Jamaica Plain   Runs the gamut from expensive homes surrounding Jamaica Pond and the Arnold Arboretum to low-cost housing and triple-deckers in the more densely populated areas. Its diverse ethnic population, Center Street shopping, and good public transportation (MBTA Orange Line, Arborway Green Line, and buses) make it popular with renters. A two-bedroom apartment averages about $500.

Mattapan   A small, densely populated neighborhood close to the exclusive town of Milton. Racially integrated and multiethnic, it has many triple-deckers and two-family houses. A two-bedroom apartment rents for $350, but transportation is somewhat cumbersome. Buses connect to the MBTA Orange Line and trolleys connect to the Red Line.

North End   An urban residential area with a predominantly Italian-American population. Hanover is the main street, with many bakeries, restaurants, and typical neighborhood stores. It's only a short walk to downtown Boston and Faneuil Hall Marketplace via the pedestrian tunnel under the JFK Expressway, but apartments in this very close-knit community are hard to come by. When available, you might find a one-bedroom for $400, but you might have to share the bathroom. (MBTA Green Line.)

Roslindale   Separated from Hyde Park by the expansive Arnold Arboretum (part of Boston's "emerald necklace" park system) is this older, stable, family-type community. Most of its one- and two-family houses are owner-occupied, and a two-bedroom apartment averages about $400. There are several shopping areas. The MBTA buses connect to the Orange and Green Lines.

South Boston   This famous Irish stronghold, immortalized by song and legend, has super recreational facilities — beaches, sailing, fishing, and ice skating — that make it popular with young and old alike. There are many older two- and three-story wooden

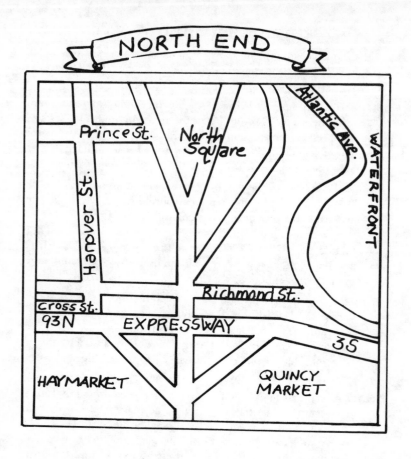

NORTH END

Princess St.

North Square

Hanover St.

Atlantic Ave.

WATERFRONT

Richmond St.

Cross St.

93N

EXPRESSWAY

3S

HAYMARKET

QUINCY MARKET

houses and also many row houses with two-bedroom apartments renting for about $400 a month and up. Good public transportation (buses, MBTA Red Line); but if you drive, the Southeast Expressway can be a commuter's nightmare.

South End Not to be confused with South Boston, this area has been undergoing extensive renovation since the 1960s. Elegant old townhouses are being restored into homes and condos and a fashionable village is coming to life here. Close proximity to the Prudential Center and Copley Square puts working and shopping within easy reach. Apartments in the newly renovated buildings are expensive, a two-bedroom averaging $600; but transportation is excellent via the MBTA Red and Green Lines and buses. You'll want to be close to transportation in this neighborhood as walking around here after dark is not recommended.

Waterfront Next to Beacon Hill, this is the oldest section of the city; yet as a residential area, it is the newest. Many of the antique wharf buildings have been converted into luxury apartments and condominiums with lots of glass and exposed brick. Faneuil Hall Market, boating, tennis and swimming clubs, and modern restaurants and night spots make this area popular with young professionals. One-bedroom apartments start at $600 a month; but you can save on transportation, as you will walk to just about everything. MBTA Green, Blue, and Orange Lines are close by.

West Roxbury It has the look and feel of an outer suburb, yet it is still part of the city. Single- and two-family houses make this another family-oriented community. The country's oldest (and still one of its most coveted) private school, the Roxbury Latin School, is located here. Good recreational facilities and excellent commuting (MBTA commuter rail service, Orange Line, and buses) add to the desirability of the area. A two-bedroom apartment rents for about $450.

THE NEAR SUBURBS

Arlington Twenty to thirty minutes by frequent MBTA service; apartments start at $375.

Belmont Thirty minutes to downtown Boston by MBTA (also commuter trains); apartments start at $350.

Brookline Ten to twenty-five minutes to downtown; excellent MBTA service; apartments start at $400.

Cambridge Ten to fifteen minutes to Boston; excellent MBTA service and commuter rail service to surrounding suburbs; apartments start at $325.

Medford Twenty to thirty minutes to Boston on frequent MBTA service; apartments are scarce here and start at $350.

Milton Fifteen minutes to Boston; Eastern Mass. bus and rapid transit service to Boston; scarce rentals start at $450.

Quincy Fifteen to twenty minutes by MBTA; rentals start at $275.

Somerville Fifteen to twenty minutes to downtown on frequent MBTA bus service; apartments start at $300.

Watertown Twenty to thirty minutes to downtown Boston (ten minutes to Cambridge); apartments start at $400.

Winchester Fifteen minutes by frequent commuter trains, also express buses to downtown; apartments start at $425.

Winthrop Thirty minutes to downtown Boston, rapid transit buses connect with MBTA; apartments start at $280.

TRANSPORTATION

Getting in and out of Boston is relatively easy, but getting around once you're here is another matter. Poets and song writers have devoted hours to describing the charms or pitfalls (depending on their sentiments) of Boston's crooked streets and meandering subways. So the best advice we can offer is, whenever possible, walk. You'll probably get to your destination faster and definitely cheaper.

If, however, you plan to drive your car around the city, the most important prerequisites are patience and a sense of humor. You've undoubtedly heard some of those awful jokes about Boston drivers? Well, they're all true!

Finding a metered parking spot in downtown Boston on a weekday is rare; and parking lots, in spite of their high rates ($8 to $14 a day) are usually full by 10:00 a.m. Also, parking regulations are strictly enforced, and violations are costly.

If you are coming into the city just for a day, there are many strategically located parking lots at suburban MBTA stations. You can park your car there for a minimal fee and ride the rapid transit into town. For information call 722-3201.

MBTA

The rapid transit is the easiest and least expensive way to get around the city. The MBTA (the Massachusetts Bay Transit Authority) operates the subways, trolley buses, and commuter trains. The letter T is both a symbol and a nickname for the subway system. For transit information, call 722-3200.

It is fairly uncomplicated, consisting of only four lines, all radiating out from downtown Boston. The system is nicely color-coded on handy wallet-size cards that are available at the Park Street station, most hotels, and visitor information booths. These cards are also available in Spanish and Chinese.

For a quick study of the subway system check the map below.

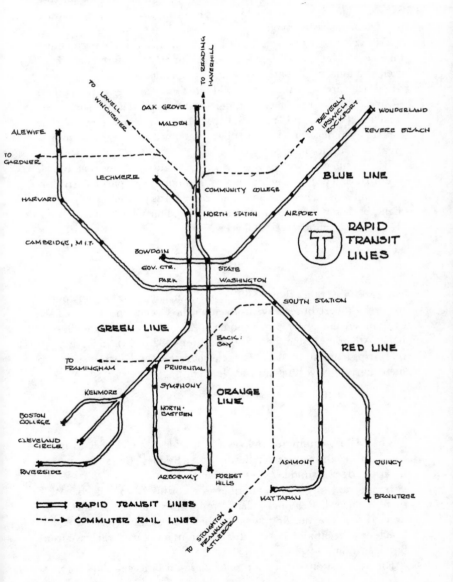

MBTA subway stations are indicated by signs with a large circled letter T at the street-level entranceway. Once down under, you'll find that the stations are usually well-lighted — and colorful. Compared to the stations in Moscow's subways or San Francisco's BART, the MBTA is a tawdry old relic, but it's not without appeal. While waiting for your car you might be entertained by a classical guitarist, a concert violinist, or a talented street-singer.

Exact change is required at surface stops of the T, but you can buy a token for 60 cents at all rapid-transit stations. On surface buses, however, you must be prepared with 50 cents' change.

The cars are quite modern — although some are newer than others — and, when you can get a seat, quite comfortable. During rush hours (8:00 to 9:00 a.m. and 4:30 to 5:30 p.m.) you can expect to stand. The cars travel underground in the subway, but once outside the downtown area, they surface to street level.

Boston subways are reasonably safe but caution is always advised. Handbag and wallet snatching is a constant problem, particularly during rush hours. There are some security guards patrolling subways at night; but after dark, you might want to heed the Checker Cab motto: "Don't take a chance, take a Checker."

BUSES

Bus services other than MBTA offer transportation to many outlying areas. These buses leave from either the Greyhound Terminal, 16 St. James Avenue near Copley Square (423-5810), or Trailways Terminal at Atlantic Avenue, near South Station (482-6620). In addition to daily trips to many areas of Massachusetts, there is daily bus service to many parts of New England and New York.

TRAINS

The MBTA commuter rail system provides train service to many communities in the Greater Boston area. Besides commuting hours, the trains operate midday, evenings, and weekends.

If you want to get to the northern or northwestern suburbs (Waltham, Concord, Reading, Salem, etc.), trains leave from North Station. If you are heading in a southern or southwestern direction (Wellesley, Needham, Norwood, Stoughton, etc.), you will leave from South Station.

For information about train schedules and fares call the Boston &

Maine Railroad (which operates the trains under the jurisdiction of the MBTA) at 227-5070 (North Station) or at 482-4400 (South Station). Consult the map below for further help.

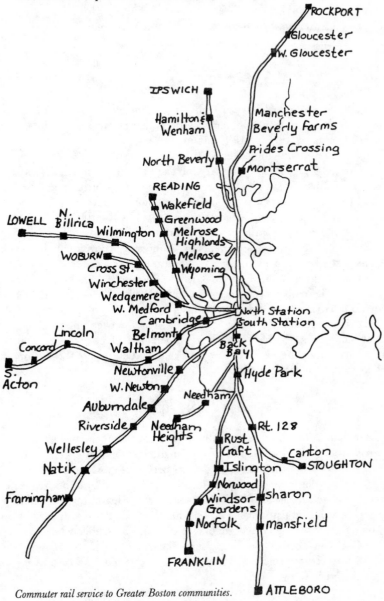

Commuter rail service to Greater Boston communities.

Amtrak, which leaves from South Station, provides frequent inter-
city service to points south — Providence, New Haven, New York,
Philadelphia, and Washington. This train stops and picks up passengers at Route 128 (Dedham/Westwood area). There is also a daily train
from South Station to Chicago that stops in Worcester, Springfield,
and Albany. For information call 482-4400.

TAXIS

Taxis can be found either cruising or at stands located in all major
shopping areas, in front of hotels, at Government Center, in the financial district, and at some MBTA stations.

If you are outside these areas you can call anyone of the following
services to be picked up: Checker Cab (536-7000), Boston Cab (536-
5010), or Town Taxi (536-5000). If you are in Cambridge there are
almost always taxis at Harvard and Central Square MBTA stations; or
for quick service call Ambassador Brattle Taxi at 492-1100.

Most of these cab companies have twenty-four-hour service and will
also deliver packages or documents to business or professional offices.
Consult the Boston Yellow Pages for additional taxi services.

Taxis charge on a meter basis. The base fare is 90 cents for the first
1/6 mile. Thereafter it is 20 cents for each additional 1/6 mile. All tolls
are added to the fare. If you are sharing a cab with another party, the
taxi driver is required by law to restart the meter at each stop.

If you feel that you have been overcharged or given poor service, you
can telephone your complaint to the Hackney Division of the Boston
Police Department, 247-4475.

CAR RENTALS

All major car-rental agencies have offices at convenient locations
throughout the city as well as at Logan International Airport. Rates
vary greatly, with some of the local firms being the most inexpensive.

If you are planning day trips to locations not served by public transportation, check the Boston Yellow Pages for a listing of car-rental
places. (A partial list is at the end of this chapter.) Rates will vary by
daily charge, mileage rate, size of car, gas, and insurance fees. Some
agencies offer weekend or overnight specials.

All auto-rental firms have a minimum age requirement which varies
from eighteen to twenty-five years.

If you are planning to rent a car and will be driving around the Boston area, it is a good idea to get a list of gas stations and repair services in this area, particularly those in Boston proper, from the rental agency.

LIMOUSINES

There are several good limousine services in the Boston area providing everything from executive transportation to sightseeing or shopping tours.

One of the most outstanding (and headed by a woman), Coopers of Boston, offers a wide variety of services. Its fourteen-passenger van can cost as little as $2.50 per person, per driving hour. A Cadillac limousine for six is $5 per person. Its chauffeur-guides are personable and knowledgeable, and many are bilingual. Coopers is at 92 State Street in Boston (482-1000).

Cap's Auto Livery is Boston's oldest chauffeured limousine service and comes well recommended. They have special rates for taking a group to dinner and theater and returning you back to your lodgings. They are located in downtown Boston at 49 North Margin Street (523-0727).

Carey of Boston (161 Broadway, Somerville, 623-8700) is part of Carey International, the nation's largest limousine-rental system. Besides local service (airport, dinner/theater, tours), they will take you anywhere in New England.

LOGAN INTERNATIONAL AIRPORT

There are approximately fifteen domestic airlines serving Boston, and eight to ten international lines, as well as several charter lines. (See partial list at end of this chapter.) In addition to their ticket and information offices at the airline terminals at Logan, many of them maintain individual offices at hotels or offices throughout the city.

Massport (Massachusetts Port Authority) shuttle buses provide service to and from all terminals, to Logan Hilton Hotel, and to the Airport Station of the MBTA Blue Line, leading to downtown Boston. Buses leave the terminals every six to twelve minutes and there is an exact change fare of 25 cents (10 cents for children).

The MBTA Blue Line into Boston will cost you an additional fare of 60 cents — so if you only have hand luggage, this is the most inexpensive and, quite often, the quickest way to get into town.

There is also a Share-A-Cab plan which you can check out at the Share-A-Cab booth usually located next to the baggage claim area.

Most downtown hotels are served by the Airways Transportation Company, which operates a limousine service to and from the airport. The charge is between $3 and $4, but be sure to check to make sure that it stops at the hotel you want. Limousines operate from 7:00 a.m. to 10:00 p.m., leaving every thirty minutes.

Taxi service to and from Logan (from downtown Boston) costs about $8 to $10, depending on time and traffic. It can also take anywhere from fifteen to forty minutes, so be sure to allow enough time.

For a complete listing of all services — taxis, buses, trains, airlines, rent-a-car agencies, and gas stations — check the Boston Yellow Pages. Here is a partial list for your convenience:

Airlines
American 542-6700
Air Canada 800-223-6161
Delta 567-4100
Eastern 262-3700
New York Air 569-8400
People's Express 523-0820
TWA 367-2800
US Air 482-3160
United 482-7900
PBA (Cape & Islands) 569-4677
Bar Harbor (Maine) 800-732-3770

Public Transportation
MBTA (days) 722-3200
Amtrak 1-800-523-5720
Gray Line Bus 426-8800
Greyhound Bus 423-5810
Trailways Bus 482-6620

Road Service
738-6900 days
731-9050 nights

Car Rental
Ajax, Logan 569-3500, Boston 542-4196
Avis, Logan 569-3300, Boston 267-5151
Budget, Logan 569-4000, Boston 266-3537
Brodie, Cambridge 491-7600
Hertz, 1-800-654-3131
National, Logan 569-6700, Boston 426-6830
Thrifty, Logan 569-6500, Boston 367-6777

2

LIFE SUPPORT
SYSTEMS

⌐⌐

RESTAURANTS

Boston, "the home of the bean and the cod," has never been particularly known for a strong emphasis on gourmet dining. For many years only a handful of restaurants here had attained celebrity status — and mostly by catering to the hearty male appetite. Most of them bore their owners' names: Jimmy's; Anthony's; Jacob Wirth's; Brandy Pete's; and, of course, Locke-Ober's, where the only woman seen within its exclusive walls was the nude portrait of Mademoiselle Yvonne above the bar.

But within the last two decades many changes have taken place. A number of outstanding women chefs — Julia Child, Joyce Chen, Madeleine Kamman, Margaret Romagnoli — began exhibiting their talents on local TV channels and created a revolution of sorts.

They, as well as many of their students, have since opened boutique-style cafes that have brought to Boston a whole new experience of fine dining. Now some of the most popular restaurants around here have names such as Rebecca's, Joyce Chen's, Tigerlilies, Annie B.'s, and Lily's. And it's not surprising that the ambiance of these restaurants is particularly suited to women.

Gone are the days when the woman traveler to Boston had to resort to room service for hassle-free dining. The restaurants listed in the following section are places where you won't find yourself seated next to the kitchen, be ignored by the waiter, or feel inhibited about returning the wine.

Most of the popular restaurants in Boston, including those in the hotels, do not accept reservations on Saturday nights. This means you

Julia Child, Boston's French chef, hosts her popular show on WGBH.

will spend a lot of time in the lounge waiting for a table. It's best to phone ahead to find one that will accept a reservation, but be sure to ask how long you will have to wait once you arrive there.

(The hotel restaurants — which include some of the best dining in town — are all listed under the individual hotels in the Accommodations section of Chapter 1. As previously mentioned, the maitre d'hotel in each is well accustomed to the solo woman traveler and you can expect the best in service and food.)

BACK BAY RESTAURANTS

Most Back Bay restaurants are located in elegant turn-of-the-century brownstones along Newbury and Boylston Streets. These were once the fashionable homes of the proper Bostonians of Victorian days.

Many of the city's finest shops, art galleries, and cultural institutions are located here as well, making it a bustling center of activity both day and night.

The Ritz-Carlton stands at the corner of Arlington and Newbury Streets, facing the Boston Public Garden. It still has the most prestigious formal dining room in town, a lounge for afternoon tea, a bar lined with banquettes for lunch or cocktails, and a ground-floor cafe overlooking Newbury Street which is a very popular breakfast spot.

Walking up Newbury (or Boylston) Street from the Garden, the cross streets are alphabetically named — Arlington, Berkeley, Clarendon, etc., ending at Kenmore Square (Massachusetts Avenue).

Most of the restaurants located here are small, boutique-style cafes; and during the warmer months (May–September) bright umbrella-tables and chairs set out on the sidewalks give a continental flair to the neighborhood.

Prices vary from inexpensive to moderate, with a few very expensive restaurants so mentioned. Many of the cafes have a menu with prices posted out front so you can get an idea of what to expect before you enter.

Annie B. Restaurant
651 Boylston St.   236-2203

Wonderful dining with a French flair amid pastel pinks and crystal. Their pastries are a treat claiming "death by chocolate" to their victims. Serving continental breakfast, lunch, dinner, and Sunday brunch. (Sun.–Wed. 11:30 a.m.–midnight; Thurs.–Sat. 11:30 a.m.–1:00 a.m.)

Cafe Florian
85 Newbury St.   247-7603

Mother and daughter own this little cafe/coffee house serving espresso, French omelettes, soups and salads, and Wiener schnitzel. It recently celebrated its twenty-fifth anniversary and is the oldest continental cafe in Boston. (Mon.–Thurs. 11:00 a.m.–11:00 p.m.; Fri. & Sat. 11 a.m.–midnight; Sun. noon–6:00 p.m.)

Casa Romera
30 Gloucester St.   536-4341

Just around the corner from Newbury Street is the best and most elegant Mexican restaurant in town. Hand-painted tiles, wrought-iron grilles, and clay pots — along with sangria, tostadas, enchiladas, pollo al cilantro, right down to the delicious coffee — make this a very Mexican experience. (Mon.–Thurs. 6:00 p.m.–10:00 p.m.; Fri. & Sat. til 11:00 p.m.; closed Sun.)

Ciro & Sal's Restaurant
500 Boylston St.   437-0500

Excellent Italian cuisine with veal and pasta as its specialties. Full bar, outdoor cafe, and Sunday brunch. Atmosphere is enhanced with burgundy hues, brick floors, and violin music. (Lunch seven days 11:30 a.m.–2:45 p.m.; dinner Mon.–Sat. 5:30–9:45 p.m.; Sun. brunch 11 a.m.–3:45.)

Charley's Eating and Drinking Saloon
344 Newbury St.   266-3000

Lively casual atmosphere and great appetizers, steak, seafood, barbecued chicken, and sandwiches. There are an outdoor cafe, "super saloon sippers," and Saturday and Sunday brunch. (Mon.–Thurs. 11:30 a.m.–midnight; Fri. 11:30 a.m.–12:30 a.m.; Sat. noon–12:30 a.m.; Sun. noon–midnight.)

Davio's
269 Newbury St.   262-4810

A very elegant, small, New York–style Italian restaurant — and very expensive. But the food is excellent and the service good. Even with reservations, you may have to wait in line. At the Piano Bar from 4:00 p.m. to 1:00 a.m., a cafe menu is offered. (Daily 11:30 a.m.–11:00 p.m.; Fri. & Sat. til 11:30 p.m.)

Friday's
26 Exeter St.   266-9040

A fun place to eat but there's almost always a waiting line. Lots of activity and quite noisy at times, especially on Friday (no kidding). The menu is endless (over 100 items), offering soups, salads, steaks, sandwiches, and great drinks. Located at the corner of Exeter and Newbury Streets. (Mon.–Thurs. 11:30 a.m.–midnight; Fri.–Sun. 11:00 a.m.–2:00 a.m.)

Great Gatsby's
300 Boylston St.   536-2626

American cuisine. Luncheon specials, great hors d'oeuvres, and Sunday champagne brunch amid an atmosphere suitable to its name. Serving lunch, dinner, and Sunday brunch; open seven days. (Sun.–Thurs. 11:30 a.m.–midnight; Fri.–Sat. 11:30 a.m.–1:00 a.m.)

Harvard Book Store Cafe
190 Newbury St.   536-0095

One of our all-time favorite spots for eating alone. It's a restaurant and a bookstore, so there's plenty of reading material around, and no rush. Light meals — salads, sandwiches, pâtés — or full-course veal, fish, and pasta. Aperitifs, beer, and wine. (Mon.–Sat. 8:00 a.m.–11:00 p.m.; closed Sun.)

La Croissant
112 Newbury St.   267-1122

Pint-size restaurant serving croissants, sandwiches, home-baked items, and quiche. Lack of room makes take-out to the Public Garden more enjoyable. (Open 7:00 a.m.–7:00 p.m. seven days a week.)

L'Espalier
30 Gloucester St.   262-3023

One of Boston's top-rated restaurants and rightly so. You'll dine in simple elegance — white linens, dried flowers, and superb food. Try the "menu degustation": small servings of four different dishes served Monday–Thursday only. (Mon.–Sat. 6:00 p.m.–10:30 p.m.)

Magic Pan Creperie
47 Newbury St.   267-9315

Famous for its crepes served with various fillings; also steak, fettucini, and soups and salads. There are Sunday brunch, a nonsmoking section, and desserts made from San Francisco's popular Ghirardelli chocolate. Continental breakfast is served outside, weather permitting. (Mon.–Thurs. 11:00 a.m.–10:00 p.m.; Fri. & Sat. 11:00 a.m.–midnight; Sun. til 10:00 p.m.)

Pomme de Terre
230 Newbury St.   266-0421

Gourmet delights and take-out too. The owner offers you a taste of his specialties of the day. Homemade pastries and sweets, good food, reasonable prices, and very friendly atmosphere. Classical music is often played by live musicians at lunch hour. (Mon.–Fri. 7:45 a.m.–8:30 p.m.; Sat. 9:00 a.m.–6:00 p.m.; Sun. 11:00 a.m.–6:00 p.m.)

The Women's Educational and Industrial Union
356 Boylston St.   536-5651

A great place for women to enjoy lunch. Set above the shop itself, this cafeteria-style tearoom offers coffee and muffins at 10:00 a.m. and lunch (assorted sandwiches, salads, and desserts) from 11:45 a.m. until 3 p.m. Open every day but Sunday.

BEACON HILL RESTAURANTS

There are several really fine restaurants on Beacon Hill, providing everything from a quick cup of morning coffee and pastry, or a casual lunch, to a leisurely gourmet dinner. Most of them are small, intimate places and many have an impressive list of take-out meals.

For a special treat, there's Deluca's Market, which has been catering to the neighborhood since 1819, and where you can get all the ingredients you'll need for a picnic — weather permitting — in the Public Garden across the way.

Here are a few of the favorite eating spots of several women we polled who live, work, or shop on the Hill.

Another Season
97 Mt. Vernon St.   367-0880

An elegant yet small restaurant right next to historic Louisburg Square. The nouvelle cuisine menu changes biweekly and it's a comfortable place to lunch or dine alone. (Lunch Tues.–Sat. noon–2:00 p.m.; dinner Mon.–Sat. 5:45–10 p.m.)

Bel Canto Restaurant
42 Charles St.   523-5575

Award-winning small Italian restaurant that's casual and friendly and has a complete take-out service. (Open seven days 11:00 a.m.– 11:00 p.m.; Mon. & Tues. til 10:30 p.m.)

The Charles Restaurant
75 Chestnut St.   523-4477

A cozy yet sophisticated restaurant (one of the oldest on the Hill) with a Northern Italian menu. It's popular with Beacon Hill Brahmins and politicians, and suburbanites too (it has valet parking). (Mon.– Thurs. 5:00–10:00 p.m.; Fri. & Sat. 5:00–11:00 p.m.)

Hampshire House
84 Beacon St.   227-9600

A turn-of-the-century Boston mansion where you can overlook the Public Garden during lunch or dinner (or brunch on the weekend). The Bull & Finch Pub is crowded and noisy but fun; it's famous for being the model for the TV sitcom, "Cheers!" (Lunch 11:45–2:30; dinner 6:00–10:30.)

The Hungry I
71 1/2 Charles St.   227-3524

Step down into one of the most romantic spots in Boston. Fresh flowers, candlelight, and delicious continental cuisine complete the picture. (Lunch 12:00–3:00; dinner 6:00–10:00 p.m.; Sun. brunch 11:00 a.m.–3:00 p.m.; closed Mon.)

Rebecca's
21 Charles St.   742-9747

The best of everything — for breakfast (opens at 7:30 a.m.), lunch (including boxed or picnic baskets), and dinner (until midnight). Complete take-out service; and if you need catering for a business meeting, reception, or wedding, Rebecca is well experienced in handling all such affairs. (Open daily 7:30 a.m.–midnight; Sun. brunch 11:30–4:00.)

Romano's Bakery and Coffee Shop

89 Charles St. 523-8704

A real neighborhood-style cafe where you can get quick service or take time for a friendly chat over coffee and pastry or salad and a sandwich. (Open seven days 7:30 a.m.–10:30 p.m.)

Pasta Pronto

144 Charles St. 367-5766

Delicious Italian dishes to take out or to eat right there. One woman we know went there every night for a week to bring her Italian mother a special dinner while she was a patient in the Mass. Eye and Ear Infirmary (right around the corner on Cambridge Street). (Mon.–Sat. 11:00 a.m.–7:00 p.m.; closed Sun.)

Tigerlilies

23 Joy St. 523-0609

If you want the real flavor of Beacon Hill, look for this tiny old-world charmer nestled away in a courtyard where you can dine outside in the summer or sit inside by a roaring fire in the winter. Nouvelle American, homemade soups, and vegetarian fare are among their specialties. (Lunch Mon.–Fri. 11:30–3:30; dinner Sun.–Thurs. 5:00–10:00 p.m., Fri. & Sat. til 11:00 p.m.; Sun. brunch 11:30–3:30.)

CHINATOWN RESTAURANTS

Some of the best Chinese restuarants are found outside of Boston's Chinatown. Joyce Chen's, for example, is at 390 Rindge Avenue and 302 Massachusetts Avenue — both in Cambridge. Joyce opened the first Mandarin-Szechuan restaurant in the United States and was soon appearing in her own program on PBS teaching the public how to cook Chinese meals.

Colleen's Chinese Cuisine at 792 Main St., also in Cambridge, is another truly wonderful restaurant with authentic dishes from Peking, Szechuan, and Hong Kong, prepared by Colleen herself — or one of the members of her large East China family.

But if you're shopping in Chinatown or going to the theater (the theater district is close by), you may want to try one of the restaurants here. We do not, however, recommend walking around Chinatown at night.

China Pearl

9 Tyler St. 426-4338

In the heart of Chinatown on Tyler Street and on the second floor, this is a restaurant where the neighbors come for their special celebrations — graduations, weddings, birthdays. They offer an ample menu filled with both the ordinary and the exotic Chinese dish. (Open seven days 11:30 a.m.–2:00 a.m.)

Golden Palace Restaurant
14–20 Tyler St.   423-4565

This is a new restaurant (in a very old Chinese restaurant location) just across from the China Pearl. The cuisine is Hong Kong, as is the decor, with sparkling china and glassware — and napkins and table-cloths. (Daily 9:00 a.m.–2:00 a.m.)

The Imperial Teahouse
70 Beach St.   426-8543

Authentic Cantonese cuisine and most noted for its Dim Sum. Try the lemon duck or chicken or vegetarian dishes. (Daily 9:00 a.m.–2:00 a.m.)

DOWNTOWN CROSSING RESTAURANTS

Good restaurants in the downtown area are scarce, so if you find yourself shopping or between meetings here at lunchtime you may want to walk the few extra steps up to Bosworth Street to the Cafe Marliave or around the corner to the Parker House.

Cafe Marliave
10–11 Bosworth St.   423-6340

This intimate, European-style restaurant is built on the site of the residence of the royal governors of Massachusetts Bay Colony (1716–1776), and the original "Province Steps" remain. The food, Italian-American, is above average; and once a week, usually, they serve homemade lasagna which is excellent. (Mon.–Sat. 11:00 a.m.–10:00 p.m.)

Cafe Tremont
Corner of Tremont & School Sts.   227-8600

Housed in the Parker House Hotel lobby, this is a great place for a quick breakfast (complimentary morning newspaper), lunch (good salad bar), or dinner (extensive menu). If you're really in a hurry or meeting someone, you might try the lobby of the Parker House, where coffee, tea, and croissants are served in the morning and light sandwiches and desserts in the afternoon. (Lunch 11:30–3:30; dinner 5:00–11:00 p.m.; open seven days.)

Filene's Restaurants
Filene's Department Store

There are three restaurants in Filenes — The Greenery (357-2646) and the Pub (357-2640) on the eighth floor, and A New Leaf (357-2040) on the fourth floor. All are open Monday through Saturday from 11:00 a.m. to 3:00 p.m., with the Pub open to 6:00 p.m. on the nights that the store is open.

Take-Out Food

There are several small take-out food stores along Winter Street where you can pick up a sandwich or a salad and cross over to the Common (weather permitting) for an enjoyable lunch. There's always plenty of entertainment here — sidewalk musicians, singers, mimes, magicians, or just plain characters to watch.

Salads Plus (soups and sandwiches), Au Bon Pain (French bakery), Paris Croissant Inc., Fortune Cookie (Chinese take-out), and Warburton's Bakery are just a few of the places where you can get fast take-out service on Winter Street. But don't forget Bailey's — Boston's most famous ice cream store — which also serves sandwiches. It's located at 26 Temple Place, 74 Franklin St., and in Faneuil Hall in the Marketplace.

MARKETPLACE RESTAURANTS

Probably one of the biggest decisions you'll have to make when visiting Faneuil Hall and Quincy Market is choosing where to eat lunch and/or dinner.

The food concessions located in Quincy Market offer every imaginable type of food (shish kebab, pasta, bagels, Boston baked beans, and baklava, to name a few). Once you've fought the crowds and decided what creative delicacy to try, you can then walk around eating, as so many do, or find a spot to sit down.

The restaurants, though, are just as varied and are open later in the evening. We suggest making reservations, when possible, for most of these are quite popular.

Cityside
Quincy Market   742-7390

Being located in such a convenient spot makes Cityside a perfect meeting spot and a terrific place for lunching alone (lots of interesting sights). Their "lighter fare" menu suggests half a melon with Haagen-Dazs sherbet or fresh vegetables and dip. There are soups and salads, sandwiches, and entrees. (Sun.–Thurs. 11:30 a.m.–10:00 p.m.; Fri. & Sat. 11:30 a.m.–midnight.)

Crickets
South Market   227-3434

Its year-round dining area in the Palm Court has a sunny atmosphere even on a dismal rainy day. Crickets is a fine, leisurely place serving luncheon specialties, soups and salads, and a tempting seafood quiche. The upstairs dining room is a bit more formal, serving entrees such as veal fettucini, steak, and seafood. (Lunch 11:00–2:00; dinner 5:00–10:00 p.m.; Sun. brunch 11:00 a.m.–3:45 p.m.)

Guadalaharry's, A Great Mexican Place
Behind North Market (20 Clinton St.)   720-1190

Behind its great wooden doors you'll find Mexican tiled floors and straw fans and hear singing bandoliers "cha-cha-cha" over the sound system. The lunch menu has six mini-lunch plates, while dinner includes enchiladas, tostadas, nachos, and quesadillas. Margaritas are served by the glass or mega-liter. (Open 11:00 a.m.–midnight, seven days.)

Houlihan's
Quincy Market Area (60 State St.)   367-6377

Besides the miles of nostalgic paraphernalia on the walls, the luscious plants, and the Tiffany-style lamps, you'll find a menu crammed full of a variety of great food. Some items are sandwiches, hamburgers, nachos, and pasta. The Sunday brunch includes a bottomless glass of champagne for 99 cents. (Weekdays 11:00 a.m.–11:00 p.m.; til midnight on weekends.)

Landmark Inn
North Market   227-9660

The Café at the Inn offers open-air dining with nightly live entertainment and serves a menu of salads, sandwiches, and hamburgers. Downstairs at the nautical Thompson's Chowder House, you'll find a seafood menu and a raw bar that is hard to tear yourself away from. On the top level of the Landmark Inn is the elegant Wild Goose Restaurant where the menu consists mostly of game. Examples are Wild Goose mixed salad, marinated leg of lamb, and sauteed breast of Muscovy duck. (Generally, all three restaurants are open from 11:30 a.m.–11:00 p.m.)

Lily's
Quincy Market   nights 227-4242
                              days 227-3434

Lily's year-round outdoor Cafe offers soups, salads, sandwiches, and entrees. Downstairs at Lily's formal restaurant, French/continental entrees such as veal Oscar and shrimp scampi are served. Be sure to check out the Piano Bar, which can be heard throughout the Marketplace. (Lunch Mon.–Fri. 12:00–2:00; dinner Mon.–Sat. 5:30–10:00 p.m.)

The Romagnoli's Table
North Market   367-9114

Single places are set at the counter for the individual diner. The dishes are Northern Italian, from antipasti to soups and salads, to finally, the entree. Mr. and Mrs. Romagnoli are known for their cooking show on TV. (Lunch 11:30–3:30; dinner 6:00–10:00 p.m.)

The Salty Dog
Quincy Market   742-2094

For anyone who enjoys a quick beer and hors d'oeuvres, this is definitely the place to go. They have an excellent raw bar, a retail counter to buy fish to take with you, and a small indoor and outdoor restaurant serving a variety of seafood. (Mon.–Sat. 11:30 a.m.–10:00 p.m.; Sun. 11:30 a.m.–8:00 p.m.)

Seaside
South Market   742-8728

This sister to Cityside offers family dining in Faneuil Hall. It's fun, it's lively, and it's reasonably priced. The menu includes salads, sandwiches, and entrees. There is Sunday brunch; outside dining; and, usually, a line. (Lunch 11:30–4:45; dinner Mon.–Wed. 5:00 p.m.– 11:00 p.m., til 12:30 Thurs.–Sat.; Sun. brunch 11:30–4:15; Sun. dinner 4:30–10:30.)

NORTH END RESTAURANTS

Many of the best cooks in the North End are women and the names of the best restaurants here reflect that. Whether it's Felicia's, Florence's, or Mother Anna's, you'll most likely find the namesake right out in the kitchen cooking up her own special version of a delicious Italian dish.

Most of these restaurants have been in business for a long time, in the same locations, and have so many regular customers that it's just one big happy family scene at dinner time. No one stands on ceremony here either, and even with a reservation for dinner, you can expect to be kept waiting. But the lines are usually quite friendly and you're sure to get lots of advice on just what to order.

The North End is thought of as one of the safest neighborhoods in Boston. However, if you're going there to dine alone at night, you might just as well get there early. There is virtually no parking in the North End so it's best to plan on taking a taxi to and from the restaurant.

Felicia's
145A Richmond St. (up one flight)   523-9885

This is one of the most popular restaurants here. It's a favorite with celebrities too; Dolores and Bob Hope wouldn't think of eating anywhere else when they're in town. (Mon.–Sat. 5:00–10:15 p.m.; Sun. 2:00–9:30 p.m.)

Florence's
190 North St.   523-4480

She makes a great Italian dish called *braciolettine*, which is a combination of veal, ham, and cheese covered with a delicious mushroom sauce and served with crusty home-baked bread. (Lunch 12:00–3:00; dinner 5:00–11:00 p.m.; open seven days.)

"Fabulous" Joe Tecce's Ristorante
53 North Washington St.   742-6210

This place is so well known and such a favorite with Bostonians (in spite of the drooping plastic grapes) that Joe doesn't even have a sign out front. His specialty, steak-a-la-Mafia, is less dangerous than it sounds. (Seven days, 11:30 a.m.–11:30 p.m.)

Mother Anna's
211 Hanover St.   523-8496

Right across the street from the crowded European Restaurant (which is also good, but noisier and busier). Felicia's mother is proprietor here and makes the best fettucini Alfredo around. (Mon.–Sat. 5:00–11:00 p.m.; Sun. 3:00–11:00 p.m.)

Regina's
11½ Thatcher St.   227-0765

If you like pizza, this is the place to come. (Mon.–Sat. 11:00 a.m.–midnight; Sun. 3:00 p.m.–midnight.)

Villa Francesca
150 Richmond St.   367-2948

Across the street from Felicia's, Francesca's has considerably more ambiance. Veal Marsala is a specialty here, as well as several chicken dishes. Also, the cannoli, if you can make room for dessert, is the best in the North End. (Mon.–Thurs. 5:00–10:30 p.m.; Fri. & Sat. til 11:00 p.m.; Sun. 4:00–10:00 p.m.)

Along with shops for subs, pizza, and pastry, there are several Italian grocery stores along Hanover and Salem Streets where you can get all the ingredients you will need for putting your own meal or picnic together.

SOUTH END RESTAURANTS

The South End has been undergoing a great deal of renovation, and the charm of many of its nineteenth-century brick townhouses is being restored. The area borders the theater district and the Prudential Center, and each of the restaurants listed below is convenient to one or the other.

Cafe Amalfi
8–10 Westland Ave.   536-6396

If you're attending a concert at Symphony Hall, this is the best place to dine. It's only a block away from Symphony Hall and offers an extensive menu of reasonably priced Italian dishes. House specialties include chicken piccata, fettucini Alfredo, and many veal, seafood, and meat dishes. (Lunch on Fri. only 11:30–3:00; dinner Mon.–Sat. 5:00–10:30 p.m., Sun. 4:30–9:00 p.m.)

Nick's
100 Warrenton St.   482-0930

This has long been Boston's most popular before- and after-theater restaurant; all the major theaters are within an easy walking distance. Specializes in roast beef and steaks and some good Italian dishes. (Mon.–Sat. 11:30 a.m.–11:30 p.m.; Sat. 4:30–11:30 p.m.)

St. Botolph Restaurant
99 St. Botolph St.   266-3030

Named for the patron saint of Boston, this congenial little restaurant in one of the South End's remodeled townhouses specializes in continental cuisine featuring daily selections of fresh fish. (Lunch 12:00–2:30, Sat.–Sun. 11:00–3:00; dinner 6:00–10:30 p.m. Fri. & Sat., 6:00–midnight.) A light menu in the cafe is served Sat. & Sun. 5 p.m.–midnight.

The 57 Restaurant
200 Stuart St.   423-5700

An elegant and classy restaurant that serves American/continental food. It's particularly known for prime rib and steaks, but good fish and Greek dishes are also served here. (Daily 11:30 a.m.–11:30 p.m.)

WATERFRONT RESTAURANTS

There are so many sights and so many things to do along the waterfront (the Aquarium, the Marketplace, the Harbor Cruises) that it would be very easy to sightsee right through the eating hour. The restaurants along here, though, are particularly lively and noteworthy.

Bay Tower Room
60 State St., 33rd Floor   723-1666

The absolute ultimate in fine dining in Boston. Gourmet food (continental) and the best view (thirty-three floors up) of Boston at night make this tops in more ways than one. This is a private club during the day and reservations for dinner are a must. (Dinner only, 5:00–11:00 p.m.; closed Sun.)

The Chart House
60 Long Wharf   227-1576

The restaurant is housed in the oldest standing commercial building in Boston and close to the scene of the famous Boston Tea Party. This is a typical steak house with lots of plants, exposed brick for decor, and lots of enthusiastic waiters and waitresses saying "Hi, my name is. . . ." (Dinner only, Mon.–Thurs. 5:00–11:00 p.m.; Fri. 5:00–midnight; Sat. 4:30–midnight; Sun. 3:30–10:00 p.m.)

Stella's of Boston
74 East India Row   227-3559

While something was lost when Stella moved a few years ago from the North End to this classy new waterfront location, the restaurant is still worth a visit. A very complete Italian menu offers a variety of dishes. While the food is not up to Felicia's, there is the good view of Boston Harbor to make up the difference. (Mon.–Thurs. 11:30–10:00 p.m.; Sat. 4:00–11:00 p.m.; Sun. noon–10:00 p.m.)

The Winery
Lewis Wharf   523-3994

Similar in decor and food to the Chart House, this large restaurant is in the restored Pilot House on Lewis Wharf. Servings here are hefty and you may want to settle for the very generous salad bar instead of a whole meal. (Lunch Mon.–Fri. 11:30–4:00; lunch Sat. noon–4:00; lunch Sun. 2:00–6:00 p.m. Dinner Mon.–Thurs. 5:00–10:00 p.m.; dinner Fri. & Sat. 5:00–midnight; dinner Sun. 2:00–10:00 p.m.)

SERVICES

INSTANT SERVICE

Just inside the Boston Telephone Book is a long list of community service numbers to put you in touch with both government and non-profit organizations that provide information on a variety of community services in and around Boston.

Here are some useful dial-it services for instant information.

Arts Line	437-1660
Boston Events	267-6446
Bostix	723-5181
Concertline (WEEI)	931-1616
Concert Line (WCOZ)	931-1502
Time	N-E-R-V-O-U-S
Weather (local)	936-1234
Weather (out-of-state)	Area Code 936-1212
Women's USA Hotline	1-800-221-4945
Visitor's Service	267-6446

Travelers' Aid Society
312 Stuart St., Boston   542-7286

Information, personal counseling, and referral services for travelers. As part of a nationwide chain it provides help for women with children traveling alone, aged or handicapped travelers, newcomers, and travelers encountering unexpected difficulties.

PERSONAL DETAILS

Beauty Salons

Most of the hotels have very good salons that cater to guests, but there are also many excellent ones along Newbury Street: L'Elegance, 103 Newbury (536-1290), also has a shop at the Prudential Center, 804 Boylston (536-4890); The Studio, 164 Newbury (247-1777); and Janet T. Cormier, 279 Newbury (266-0300). There are also salons at Jordan

Marsh (357-3000); Filene's (357-2144); Lord & Taylor (262-6000); and Saks (262-8500). Geneses Salon, 150 South Market, Faneuil Hall (720-4555) also has a makeup bar and showers, as well as exercise classes and sauna (open 8:00 a.m.–8:00 p.m. Mon.–Fri., 9:00 a.m.– 3:00 p.m. Sat.).

Health and Athletic Facilities

The Boston Park Plaza Hotel has a health club with sauna, steam, and massage (542-6861). The Women's Athletic Club of the Boston YWCA (536-0991) and the Cambridge YWCA (491-6050) both have pools and a full line of athletic facilities. The Boston Athletic Club, Inc. (269-4300) has a pool, saunas, and whirlpool. The Workout Loft, 91 Newbury Street (437-7131), offers classes on a drop-in basis for intense head-to-toe workout including aerobic exercises; shower facilities available. (See also Sports and Fitness, page 156.)

Repair Services

There are shoe repair shops in both the Little Building at the corner of Boylston and Tremont Streets (426-6244) and the Park Square Building at 31 St. James Street (426-6480); also Santacross at 10 Temple Place (426-6978) and Boston Bootmakers, 115 Summer Street (523-3140).

If the strap breaks on your luggage, you can try M&M Luggage Repair at 611 Washington Street (426-9147).

Eyeglasses can be repaired at Parelli Optical, one-hour service (542-7005), or Pearle Vision Center (523-0272) at several downtown locations; and Filene's repairs jewelry (357-2201).

Dry cleaning/tailor: Prudential One-Hour Cleaners is at three locations (338-7271); Plymouth Tailors, 59 Temple Place (426-7175), does both alterations and repairs; and Sarni (247-7302) has seven locations all over town.

BUSINESS SERVICES

Secretarial Services

Back Bay Typing service, 115 Newbury Street (266-4995); Bette James and Associates, Harvard Square (661-2622); A-plus Secretarial Service, Cambridge (491-2200).

Stenography

The Skill Bureau (423-2986) on Tremont Street in Boston.

Quick Copy

Sir Speedy offers free pickup and delivery in two locations: downtown (227-2237) and Prudential (267-9711); and Copy Cop is at the Pru (267-9267) and in the financial district (367-2738).

Messenger

Bell Mercury Messenger Service, 125 Pearl Street (426-9293), will deliver your small package or documents, Boston and Cambridge.

Photography

Photo World offers one-hour service and is located in four handy spots: downtown (423-4819), Pru (266-6556), and the financial district (423-4818) and Cambridge (497-0731). Bromfield Camera Co. does repairs, 10 Bromfield Street (426-5230).

MARY BAKER EDDY
1821–1919

Mary Baker Eddy, founder of the Christian Science religion and The Christian Science Monitor *newspaper.*

One Boston woman (although born in Bow, New Hampshire) who has truly been given the distinction of being called a "founding mother" is Mary Baker Eddy. She founded the Christian Science religion and her First Church of Christ, Scientist, chartered in Boston in 1879, is known throughout the world as The Mother Church.

She firmly believed in a "Father-Mother God," and a high percentage of her followers have always been women. Her "spiritual interpretation" of the Lord's Prayer begins, "Our Father-Mother God, all harmonious, Adorable One. . . "

As a child and throughout the first half of her long life, Mary was plagued by poor health. Constantly searching for cures, and having heard of the success in mental healing of Dr. Phineas Parkhurst Quimby, she went to him for treatment. She was temporarily restored to good health by his methods and for a time was greatly influenced by his theories.

When Dr. Quimby died, Mary, at age forty-five, came to understand healing in a very different, Christian framework and became a teacher and healer herself. She began to write her now famous book, *Science and Health* with *Keys to the Scriptures*, on her own new approach to religion and healing. Printed privately in 1875 without benefit of publishers' promotion or booksellers' interest, it has gone through hundreds of printings and has sold millions of copies throughout the world.

In 1907, when a lawsuit was brought against Mrs. Eddy by members of her family questioning her competence to run her own affairs, she demonstrated her lucidity by granting interviews to three of the outstanding newspapermen of the day. Their overwhelming endorsement of this "remarkable woman" was best summed up by William E. Curtis of the *Chicago Record-Herald* who wrote, "I have never seen a woman eighty-six years of age with greater physical or mental vigor." The suit was dropped.

The adverse publicity from this trial so disturbed her, however, that she promptly set about founding her own newspaper. Today that paper, *The Christian Science Monitor*, is a highly influential and respected national daily newspaper.

The Christian Science Center, a beautiful complex of buildings set off by a long reflecting pool with fountains and flowers, has several interesting daily tours available. A unique experience is walking through the inside of a huge stained-glass globe, the Mapparium, and listening to whispered echoes.

Another tribute to Mary Baker Eddy is the magnificent Longyear Estate in Brookline (120 Seaver Street, 277-8943). Here you can tour a hundred-room turn-of-the-century house (a spacious stone mansion that was moved from Michigan to Brookline by the Longyears, devoted followers of Eddy) containing portraits, photos, manuscripts, and personal possessions of Mrs. Eddy. It is open daily from 9:00 to 5:00 (it closes earlier in the winter), and you can reach it by taking the T to Kenmore Square and then the Chestnut Hill bus to Fisher Avenue.

EMERGENCY AND SAFETY

Unfortunately, Boston cannot boast about its crime rate — it is high. But this does not mean that you have to walk in fear on the streets. There are certain areas where most crimes occur and these, of course, should be avoided. Chances are you wouldn't want to go there anyway. They include such places as the Combat Zone (lower Washington and Tremont Streets) and parts of Dorchester and Roxbury, as well as the obvious places after dark — the parks, the Common, the Orange Line on the subway, any dark alley or side street, and multilevel garages.

Women in Boston and Cambridge have held many marches and demonstrations to "take back the night"; but so far, we're all still taking lots of necessary precautions. Here are some suggestions from the Boston Police Department:

Before you leave your hotel or place of business, know where you are going and how to get there.

If you are lost, look for a police officer, meter maid, or shopkeeper, and ask them for directions.

Walk with confidence. If you think you are being followed, stop at the nearest shop or restaurant and ask for help.

Don't let your handbag swing loose from your shoulder, and don't hang it over the arm of a chair in a restaurant.

Keep all doors locked — car, hotel room, or apartment.

If an emergency should occur, you can dial one number for Ambulance, Fire, or Police: 911 or "0" for the operator. Always give the following information:

Emily Green Balch, the second American woman to win the Nobel Peace Prize, was born in Jamaica Plain in 1867.

1. Nature of emergency.
2. State and city you are calling from.
3. House, hotel, or building number and street name.
4. Exact location.
5. Telephone number you are calling from.

The following crisis numbers are answered on a twenty-four-hour basis:

Alcohol Problems	524-7884 (AIR — referral service)
Drug Abuse	569-8792 (Anonymous Hotline)
Personal Crisis	267-9150 (Project Place)
Poison	232-2120 (Children's Hospital)
Psychiatric Emergency	726-2994 (Mass. General Hospital)
	726-2000
Rape	492-7273 (Rape Crisis Center)
Suicide	247-0220 (Samaritans)

Some of the best medical facilities in the world are located in Boston; here are some of the top ones for emergency service:

Beth Israel Hospital	735-3337
Brigham & Women's Hospital	732-5636
Children's Hospital	735-6000
Mass. General Hospital	726-2000
Mass. Eye & Ear Infirmary	523-7900
New England Medical Center	956-5566
St. Elizabeth Hospital	782-7000
Tufts Dental Clinic	956-6828

Medical prescriptions are available around the clock at Phillips Drug Store, 155 Charles Street, Boston (523-1028, 523-4372).

Information Center for Individuals with Disabilities (ICID)

20 Park Plaza, Room 330	727-5540
Boston, MA 02116	or toll-free 800-462-5015

This service provides information and referrals for disabled persons and their families, friends, and service providers. They will answer questions about accessibility, finances, employment, education, housing, recreation, transportation, and more. Hours are 9:00 to 5:00 Monday to Friday. They are a nonprofit organization and there are no charges for their services.

NETWORKING

WOMEN'S ORGANIZATIONS

No sooner had the Puritans settled in Boston than the first women's organization was formed. In the early 1630s, Anne Hutchinson gathered together a group of neighborhood women to discuss the sermons of the Reverend John Cotton. Anne did not agree with John's theology and the discussions became quite lively. The meetings in fact became so popular and insightful that even the men in the community, including the governor, began to take part.

Unfortunately Anne was soon banished from Boston as a heretic; but in spite of this, women's religious organizations continued to flourish. It wasn't until the 1770s, however, that women actually organized for political reasons.

At this time, women as well as the men in the colony were becoming increasingly agitated by the constant injustices of the British government, particularly the heavy tax on imported goods. The women began to gather in groups to spin and weave material for their own and their families' garments rather than wear the imported British ones.

They gave up drinking and serving tea because of the tea tax, and drank coffee instead. When one of them discovered that a local mer-

Boston women, carrying a banner in memory of Julia Ward Howe, march in a woman suffrage parade in Washington, DC on March 13, 1913.

chant was hoarding coffee in order to drive the price up, over one hundred women marched en masse to the warehouse, where they publicly exposed the culprit.

The rest is history. Abolitionists, suffragists, temperance advocates, and on into the modern age of NOW and 9 to 5 — women's groups have proliferated here. Whether social, political, religious, or educational, organizations of women have dedicated their efforts over the centuries toward improving the quality of life for everyone in this city.

The following directory is by no means comprehensive but only representative of the scope and variety of some of the current groups, projects, and activities for women in and around the city. Most of the organizations are in touch with the vast network of resource and referral opportunities available to women wishing to connect with one another for either personal or professional reasons. So if you don't find the service you are looking for listed here, try one of the college and university Women's Centers below for additional information.

BUSINESS

New England Women Business Owners (NEWBO)
4 Brattle St., Suite 306
Cambridge, MA 02138   492-4682

The purpose of NEWBO is "To establish and maintain women business owners as a visible and powerful force in the American business community." It offers the woman entrepreneur visibility, dynamic speakers, management workshops, publications, a speakers' bureau, procurement assistance, and legislative clout. It not only acts as a personal network for business women but connects with many other business organizations in the state.

The Women's Network
Middlesex Community College
Division of Community Services
Springs Road
Bedford, MA 07130   275-8910 ext. 291/292

The Women's Network provides its members with wider professional contacts, a forum for the exchange of ideas and information, and support as they move along their career paths. Since May of 1979 this nonprofit organization has served a broad-based group of working women in the Routes 128 and 495 high-tech area outside Boston. The membership includes women involved in high technology, social services, education, politics, the medical professions, and owners of small businesses.

CHILD CARE

Child Care Resource Center
24 Thorndike St.
Cambridge, MA 02141   547-9861

250 Stuart St., Rm 169
(U. Mass./Downtown)
Boston, MA 02116   547-9861

Child Care Resource Center, founded in 1971, provides support services to parents and child-care providers in the Greater Boston area. A nonprofit agency, it is committed to high-quality, community-based child care. Staff members provide referrals and assistance to put individuals, programs, and organizations in touch with each other. They offer technical assistance and feasibility studies for employers considering child-care supports for employees.

Family Day Care Program
276 Washington St.
Brookline, MA 02146   738-0703/0704

Family Day Care Program, the original family day-care system in New England, places children in licensed, staff-supervised homes and provides educational activities geared to each child's needs, as well as other professional support. The program also trains women to care for small groups of children in their homes. Training covers subjects ranging from nutrition to art activities to baby exercise. Basic equipment and materials are provided. Staffers visit day-care homes regularly to give advice and assistance to day-care providers.

COLLEGE AND UNIVERSITY WOMEN'S CENTERS

Most of these centers, which began in the 1970s, offer valuable assistance to students, staff, and faculty on their respective campuses, as well as to women in the larger community. They are the focus for information on women's issues, exchanges of ideas, health and counseling referrals, and access to organizations and support groups; and most have extensive libraries of women's books and resource materials.

Boston College
Women's Resource Center
McElroy Commons 213
Chestnut Hill, MA 02167   552-3489

Boston University
Women's Center
George Sherman Union, 775 Commonwealth Ave.
Boston, MA 02215   353-4240

Brandeis University
Women's Center
Sherman Student Center, South St.
Waltham, MA 02154   647-2194

Harvard College
   Women's Center
   Lehman Hall
   Cambridge, MA 02138   495-1659

Middlesex Community College
   The Women's Network
   Springs Road
   Bedford, MA 01730   275-8910, ext. 291/292

Mass. Institute of Technology
   Women's Center
   Margaret Cheney Room, 77 Mass. Ave.
   Cambridge, MA 02139   253-1000

Northeastern University
   Women's Center
   Rm. 23, Dodge, 360 Huntington Ave.
   Boston, MA 02115   437-2130

Radcliffe College
   The Mary Ingraham Bunting Institute   495-8212
   The Henry A. Murray Research Center   495-8140
   The Schlesinger Library   495-8647
   10 Garden St.
   Cambridge, MA 02138

Simmons College
   Women's Center
   451 Marlboro St.
   Boston, MA 02115   738-3298

Suffolk University
   The Women's Program Center
   41 Temple St.
   Boston, MA 02114   723-4700

University of Massachusetts (Boston)
   The Women's Center
   Harbor Campus
   Boston, MA 02125   929-7000

University of Massachusetts (Amherst)
  The Everywomen's Center
  Amherst, MA 01033   413-545-0883

Wellesley College
  Center for Research on Women, Ext. 2500   431-1453
  Wellesley, MA 02181   235-0320

Wheelock College
  The Women's Center
  200 The Riverway
  Boston, MA 02215   734-5200

EDUCATION

Women's Technical Institute
  1255 Boylston St.
  Boston, MA 02215   266-2243

The Women's Technical Institute is a private, nonprofit school, licensed by the Commonwealth of Massachusetts Department of Education and accredited by the Council for Noncollegiate Continuing Education. Its programs and services are designed to help women of all ages and background explore and qualify for technical training and employment. Training programs are short-term and job-focused. Introductory and exploratory programs are geared to developing basic skills and technical confidence as preparation for further learning.

Women's Theological Center
  400 The Fenway
  Boston, MA 02115   277-1330

The Women's Theological Center offers a one-year program of study and action from a Christian and feminist perspective. It is designed for women working for justice in social and ecclesiastical settings and for women in academic degree programs in theology and ministry. It is part of a network of women in neighborhood, church, theological, and academic communities in metropolitan Boston, New England, and across the country. They offer workshops as well.

Women's Community School
  474 Boston Ave.
  Medford, MA 02155   381-3278

Based on the philosophy that "as women we have learned many things in our lives that help ourselves, our friends, and our families," WCS offers classes where women can come together and share their special skills and information.

The Women's Center
46 Pleasant St.
Cambridge, MA 02139   354-8807

Started in 1972 and supported by private donations, foundation grants, and the hard work of hundreds of area women, this center has been the catalyst for a wide variety of community projects. Elizabeth Stone House and Transition House, now incorporated separately, began as projects here. A long list of women's groups dealing with such subjects as abortion, alcoholism, lesbianism, black feminism, literature, sports, etc. are affiliated here.

Women's Educational and Industrial Union
356 Boylston St.
Boston, MA 02116   536-5651

Started in 1877 for discussions and study, this organization pioneered in services to Boston women such as finding employment, providing a sales outlet for handmade items, and developing the first sales training program for women in the city. It has grown from a small core of volunteers to a large, fully trained and competent staff who assist and serve approximately eight thousand women and men in the community annually. Their services include the Shops (handmade items, antiques, needlepoint and knitting supplies, gift items, and a restaurant), Social Services, Homemaker Service, Career Services, Information and Referral, Counseling, and Workshops.

Women's Van
Various locations   247-4078

A mobile educational and resource center offering information on many subjects such as consumer, legal, child-care, and social services for women, as well as referral service. This van is sponsored by the Women's Information, Referral, and Education Service — a program of the Junior League of Boston, Inc.

JULIA WARD HOWE
1819–1910

Mine eyes have seen the glory of the coming of the Lord;
He is trampling out the vintage where the grapes of wrath are stored;
He hath loosed the fateful lightning of His terrible swift sword;
His truth is marching on.

Julia Ward Howe, author of
"The Battle Hymn of the Republic,"
became known as the
"Dearest Old Lady in America."

Julia Ward Howe was born in New York and came to Boston in 1841 upon her marriage to Samuel Gridley Howe, the director of the Perkins Institution for the Blind (now called Perkins School for the Blind). Considered an outsider by the Brahmins from the start, she often used her caustic wit to strike back. When passing the Charitable Eye and Ear Infirmary one day, for example, she was heard to exclaim, "Oh, I did not know there was a charitable eye or ear in Boston."

Along with her husband she was an enthusiastic abolitionist, and together they published an antislavery paper called *The Commonwealth*. Their first home was in South Boston and they named it "Green Peace." It soon became a center of antislavery activity where many prominent intellectuals and reformers of the period gathered.

Howe's early poems were published anonymously (her husband did not believe in women attracting public attention) and received little recognition. But a war poem, scribbled down in the darkness of a camp tent she was visiting during the Civil War brought her everlasting fame. It appeared in the *Atlantic* and she received a payment of four dollars. It was called "The Battle Hymn of the Republic," and today enjoys equal status with that of the national anthem.

Howe was an inveterate club woman, founding, organizing, and directing many local and national organizations. She became extremely active in the woman suffrage movement, speaking and lecturing at conventions and legislative hearings.

Her later home on Beacon Street became a meeting place for various groups, and people from all over the world came to visit her there. She continued writing and publishing long after her husband's death (he had become reconciled to her fame years before); and at the age of eighty-nine she was elected to the American Academy of Arts and Letters, the first woman to be so honored.

She lived to be ninety-one and had well earned the love and respect not only of Brahmins and all Bostonians but of a whole nation as well. The governor of Massachusetts led the dignitaries at her funeral and hundreds had to be turned away. At a memorial service at Symphony Hall over four thousand people joined in singing "The Battle Hymn of the Republic."

EMPLOYMENT

Women's Job Counseling Center
34 Follen St.

Cambridge, MA 02138   864-9097

This program provides training and a support system aimed at enabling a woman to become permanently and economically self-sufficient. It helps participants overcome concerns, raise self-esteem, and become more familiar with the scope of the work world; it identifies skills from both paid and unpaid work while setting long-range goals; it works to enhance an individual's employability and job-hunting skills; and it assists with job placement.

WICS/Job Corps Screening Office
210 Lincoln St., Room 408

Boston, MA 02111   451-1328

Women in Community Service (WICS) is a nonprofit organization contracted by the Department of Labor to recruit and screen young women for the Job Corps. The Job Corps is a federally funded residential program which provides basic education and vocational training to income-eligible youth between the ages of sixteen and twenty-two. WICS also provides a support-service network for young women after they leave, to help them identify further educational or vocational opportunities and locate health services and other social services.

9 to 5 Organization for Women Office Workers
37 Temple Place, 4th Floor
Boston, MA 02111   423-3253

This Boston-based membership organization works toward better wages and working conditions for women office workers. Their reports and studies on unfair wages and discriminatory practices in many Boston industries have resulted in positive changes in the work place, particularly in insurance companies, publishing companies, and institutions of higher education in Massachusetts.

HEALTH

Boston Women's Health Book Collective
P.O. Box 192
West Somerville, MA 02144   924-0271

The Boston Women's Health Book Collective is a women's health education and advocacy organization, perhaps best known for their two books, *Our Bodies, Ourselves* and *Ourselves and Our Children*. Since 1969 they have been actively involved in major women's health projects. The Collective operates a Women's Health Information Center in Watertown that contains books, periodicals, and extensive literature files on a wide range of topics relevant to women and health.

American Medical Women's Association (AMWA)
Asha Wallace, MD, President
2000 Washington St.   332-3293
Newton, MA 02162   444-1583

A national organization committed to enhancing the professional image of women physicians. They offer programs such as career and practice development, lifestyle management, and education in women's health issues. They also provide a referral service for women physicians in all specialties.

New England Women's Service, Inc.
1031 Beacon St.   738-1370
Brookline, MA 02146   800-682-9218

New England Women's Service, Inc. is a licensed medical facility that offers first-trimester abortions, birth control/gynecology, free pregnancy testing, and counseling.

The Bill Baird Center
673 Boylston St.
Boston, MA 02116   536-2511

The Bill Baird Center is a reproductive-health information center providing counseling and referrals for abortion and birth control. They offer free pregnancy testing on a walk-in basis from 9:00 a.m. to 5:00 p.m., Monday through Saturday.

Preterm
1842 Beacon St.
Brookline, MA 02146   738-6210

This is a licensed, nonprofit reproductive-health-care facility. Medical services offered are first-trimester abortion, gynecology/family planning, tubal ligation, and vasectomy. Counseling with all medical services.

Planned Parenthood League of Massachusetts
99 Bishop Richard Allen Drive   Administration 492-0518
Cambridge, MA 02139   Counseling 492-0777

A private, nonprofit social-service and health-education agency serving women, men, and teens in the area of reproductive health. Their services include counseling and referral, education and training, and public advocacy.

Homebirth, Inc.
P.O. Box 355, BU Station
Boston, MA 02215   965-5166

This organization provides educational services, referrals, and support for women and couples who desire an alternative to traditional hospital birth experiences.

Breast Health Center
New England Medical Center
Box 431, 171 Harrison Ave.
Boston, MA 02111   956-5757

The Breast Health Center is staffed by medical experts skilled in all aspects of breast health and breast disease. They specialize in same-day diagnostic evaluation and recommendation for treatment. The center is open to all women and you can schedule your own appointment. It also offers free educational services to groups and organizations.

LEGAL

The Women's Law Collective
187 Hampshire St.
Cambridge, MA 02139   492-5110

Women lawyers specializing in providing legal services to women in the areas of family law, bankruptcy, employment discrimination and sexual harassment, personal injury, real estate, social security, and tenant's rights.

Alliance Against Sexual Coercion (AASC)
P.O. Box 1
Cambridge, MA 02139   547-1176

AASC was formed in 1976 to fight sexual harassment at the work place. They provide services to women who are being sexually harassed, including crisis intervention and advocacy, and information about legal options. They also provide training and consultation to a variety of groups, and offer a series of publications about sexual harassment.

Women for Economic Justice (WEJ)
145 Tremont St.
Boston, MA 02111   426-9734

Originally established in 1971 as the Governor's Commission on the Status of Women, WEJ is a statewide nonprofit membership organization seeking solutions to the economic injustices facing women in Massachusetts. They work with women's organizations throughout the state to develop strategies and methods which cut across class lines to promote the interests and well-being of all women.

The Massachusetts Woman's Divorce Handbook
    56 Gun Club Lane
    P.O. Box 743
    Weston, MA 02193   891-6198

The Massachusetts Woman's Divorce Handbook is a concise guide to the legal system for women going through a divorce. Written by Attorney Isabella Jancourtz, it lists probate courts, legal aid offices, and women's resource centers.

Justice Resource Institute
    530 Atlantic Ave.
    Boston, MA 02210   482-0006

The Justice Resource Institute is a nonprofit agency formed in 1972 through the initiative of government officials and private citizens. JRI's essential mission is to work as a partner of government to achieve creative solutions to human problems.

LESBIAN

Daughters of Bilitis
    1151 Massachusetts Ave.
    Cambridge, MA 02133   661-3633

One of the largest lesbian organizations in this area. Weekly get-togethers, sports activities, dances, and dinners are sponsored by the group, and an information and counseling phone line is available. They publish America's oldest literary journal for lesbians, *Focus*, on a bimonthly basis.

Lesbian Liberation
    c/o The Women's Center
    46 Pleasant St.
    Cambridge, MA 02139   354-8807

Lesbian Liberation is a discussion group of women that meets every Thursday at 8:00 p.m. at the Women's Center in Cambridge. There is also an information, resource, and referral service by mail (address above).

Additional information regarding regularly scheduled and special lesbian activities can be found in the calendar section of *The Soujourner* and on the bulletin board at New Words Bookstore in Cambridge.

MUSIC

Women's Music Distribution Company
33 Richdale Ave.
Cambridge, MA 02139   661-0554

Women's Music Distribution Company is a New England women-owned business. The major focus is the distribution of records and tapes, along with songbooks, from over twenty-five independent record labels which feature women. As a distribution company, WMDC wholesales to well over 100 retail outlets in New England. They also do promotion through print and radio, arrange interviews, record reviews, speak to local groups, and create advertising plans.

POLITICAL

Massachusetts National Organization for Women (NOW)
81 Wyman St.
P.O. Box 123
Waban, MA 02168   965-1713

There are approximately sixteen chapters of Mass. NOW throughout the state. NOW is a nonprofit organization that assumes a leadership role in addressing all issues that affect women in this state. Recently their priorities have included lobbying in opposition to all antiabortion legislation and fighting for legislation on two insurance bills which prohibit discrimination on the basis of sex in all insurance practices. The PAC (political action committee) of NOW is raising money to support candidates who will further women's issues in this state.

League of Women Voters of Massachusetts
8 Winter St.
Boston, MA 02108   357-8380

The League is a nonpartisan organization that never supports or opposes political parties or candidates, although it does encourage members to participate in the political process. The League itself takes action on public-policy issues addressed by the League program.

Boston women exercising their newly granted right to vote in municipal elections (1893).

There are over eight thousand members in 101 local Leagues. They sponsor public forums and candidates' nights; lobby at the State House; conduct studies on local, state, and national issues; and provide information on related matters to all members and the public.

Massachusetts Caucus of Women Legislators
  Room 156, State House
  Boston, MA 02133   722-2266

The Women's Legislative Caucus was formed in 1975 when fourteen women members of the House of Representatives felt a need to band together in order to address issues of common concern. A key issue at that time was the state Equal Rights Amendment, and their unified support was the best lobbying tool for the ERA, which the Legislature voted by an overwhelming margin in its favor. The Caucus has since worked successfully on numerous issues such as the passage in 1980 of the Rape Staircasing Law. They seek to improve the status of all women in the Commonwealth through lobbying and information dissemination.

Massachusetts Women's Political Caucus
80 Broad St.
Boston, MA 02110   451-9294

This is the state chapter of the National Women's Political Caucus that supports women political candidates, lobbies for women's issues, and organizes activist women within the political parties.

The Governor's Advisory Committee on Women's Issues
State House
Boston, MA 02133   727-7853

This is a recently formed committee replacing the Governor's Commission on the Status of Women. As head of this committee, Joan A. Quinlan serves as a policy adviser to the governor, the cabinet, and key staff members on issues of importance to women.

Women's International League for Peace & Freedom (WILPF)
897 Main St.
Cambridge, MA 02139   497-6232

WILPF was founded in 1915 by Jane Addams to work for the achievement by peaceful means of "those political, economic, social, and psychological conditions throughout the world which can assure peace, freedom, and justice for all." Local branches sponsor meetings, conferences, and seminars on disarmament, civil rights, women's rights, and civil liberties. Their publication *Peace and Freedom* is published regularly, as well as pamphlets, leaflets, and other publications.

Coalition for Basic Human Needs (CBHN)
595 Mass. Ave.
Cambridge, MA 02139   497-0126

CBHN is a statewide welfare-rights organization with a self-help orientation. Their main objective is to educate and organize welfare recipients to advocate for themselves to effect change. The membership is composed exclusively of welfare recipients and former recipients, many of whom are single mothers who have to rely on welfare payments for survival. Their goals are to combat myths and stereotypes, attain a decent standard of living, improve state programs, and provide support and advocacy for recipients.

TRAVEL

Traveler's Information Exchange
356 Boylston St.
Boston, MA 02116   536-5651, ext. 46

The Traveler's Information Exchange (formerly the Women's Rest Tour Association) was founded in 1891 by two women who refused to accept the idea that "ladies" did not travel without proper escort. Over the years, over twenty-five thousand women have taken advantage of TIE's advice and services. TIE, with a worldwide membership of about one thousand, publishes an annual magazine, quarterly newsletters, and books containing lists of lodgings and restaurants all over the world that are personally recommended by members. TIE also offers a Bed and Breakfast Exchange and sponsors several programs each year.

WOMEN IN CRISIS

Casa Myrna Vazquez, Inc.
P.O. Box 18019
Boston, MA 02118   262-9581

Casa Myrna Vazquez, Inc. is a comprehensive intervention, prevention, sheltering, follow-up, and community education program with a special outreach to Hispanic, Afro-American, and West Indian families. They seek to "create a cultural environment within our South End shelter (Casa Myrna Vazquez) and our Dorchester shelter (The Mary Lawson Foreman House) which makes it possible for our guests to feel 'at home' during their time of crisis and transition."

Crittenton Hastings House
10 Perthshire Rd.
Brighton, MA 02135   782-7600

Crittenton Hastings House and its predecessor organizations have been providing services to women in crisis with unplanned pregnancies since 1836. A comprehensive program of prenatal services is provided on both a residential and a day basis. Services include individual family and group counseling, academic programs for grades six through twelve, health care, childbirth and child-care classes, nutrition classes, a group focusing on activities of daily living, arts and crafts, cooking and sewing classes, as well as social and recreational activities.

The Elizabeth Stone House
P.O. Box 15
Jamaica Plain, MA 02130   522-3417

Elizabeth Stone House is a program for women in emotional distress and their children. The program combines low-cost residential services with advocacy and support for resolving practical and emotional problems. It offers a five-month program geared for women who have been psychiatrically institutionalized, victims of violence, mothers in crisis, and other women undergoing changes and wanting additional support.

Rosie's Place
1662 Washington St.
Boston, MA 02118   536-4652

Rosie's Place in Boston's South End has been a survival center for poor and homeless women since 1974, providing free food, clothing, and emergency shelter. They are open for dinner seven days a week, and beds are offered Sunday through Friday. It is a nonprofit organization, receives no government funding, and is run by approximately eighty volunteers and four paid staff.

Transition House
P.O. Box 530, Harvard Square Station   661-7203 (hotline)
Cambridge, MA 02138   354-2676 (office)

This is a refuge for women whose lives are threatened by violence. Women and children can stay here for six weeks while obtaining emergency service. They also operate a Boston-area telephone exchange to put women in touch with other shelters when Transition House is full. They have instigated many preventive-education programs and workshops for adolescents.

Women's Alcoholism Program
    6 Camelia Ave.
    Cambridge, MA 02139   661-1316

The Women's Alcoholism Program of CASPAR Inc. (Cambridge and Somerville Program for Alcoholism Rehabilitation) provides a full range of services specifically designed to identify and meet the requirements of alcoholic women. From emergency counseling to detoxification to residential, outpatient, and after-care services, this program offers comprehensive treatment for women coping with alcohol problems.

The Boston Psychological Center for Women
    Suite 902, Statler Office Building
    20 Park Plaza
    Boston, MA 02116   542-2676

This is a professional, multiracial/ethnic group of women who have been providing psychological services to women and their families and friends since 1975. These services include individual counseling and psychotherapy (short- and long-term), couple and family counseling, career counseling, and psychological testing and evaluation. They have a twenty-four-hour answering service and are fully licensed.

Women's Counseling and Resource Center
    1555 Massachusetts Ave.
    Cambridge, MA 02138   492-8568

This center provides counseling and referral services primarily on a short-term basis for women concerned with current emotional conflicts in their lives, issues of personal growth, and the changing identity of women. The center's referral services assist women with legal problems, child care, birth control, health care, and vocational information.

Women's Resource Center
    New England Medical Center
    171 Harrison Ave., Box 1007
    Boston, MA 02111   956-5750

The Women's Resource Center is a nonprofit service organization designed by and for working women. The Center, initiated in 1981 by the Department of Psychiatry, is a joint effort of New England Medical Center and the Tufts University School of Medicine. It is a clearinghouse for women seeking knowledgeable and reliable information on general health, mental health, or life-stress issues. It is an educational resource for companies and other institutions interested in providing their employees with special programs on a variety of health-related problems.

Tapestry Counseling, Inc.
20 Sacramento St.
Cambridge, MA 02138   661-0248

This is a feminist therapy collective providing individual, group, and couples therapy to women and their families and friends. They also provide supervision and training to practicing therapists and students; conduct workshops and make presentations to various community agencies; and consult to other organizations.

COPE
37 Clarendon St.
Boston, MA 02116   357-5588

COPE is a mental-health center which provides individual/group counseling, and work- and family-management seminars. Support groups are run for pregnant women, new mothers, single mothers, mothers of toddlers, and couples. Special short-term groups such as postabortion groups, child management, etc. are also held. Individual counseling includes help with decision making, family therapy, and crisis intervention; and they maintain an extensive information and referral system.

Mass. Coalition of Battered Women Service Groups (MCBWSG)
25 West St.
Boston, MA 02111   426-8492

MCBWSG is a statewide coalition of shelters, safe-home networks, and hotlines for battered women and their children. While the Coalition office does not provide services, referrals to member programs are made. The Coalition advocates for programs for battered women and distributes *For Shelter and Beyond* (a training manual for working with women who are battered) and *A Woman's Guide to the Abuse Prevention Act*.

Battered Women's Directory
c/o The Women's Center
46 Pleasant St.
Cambridge, MA 02138   492-5630

This is a comprehensive resource and reference directory of shelters, services, and educational resources for battered women and service providers in the United States.

Community Programs Against Sexual Assault (CPASA)
Dr. Solomon Carter Fuller Mental Health Center
85 E. Newton St.
Boston, MA 02118   266-8800, ext. 296/280

CPASA is a specialized rape-prevention program within the Consultation and Education Unit of the Dr. Solomon Carter Fuller Mental Health Center. They provide consultation, education, and training on all aspects of sexual assault to agencies and interested groups; information, referral, and advocacy services to rape victims and their families; and a wide range of resource materials.

WAVAW (Women Against Violence Against Women)
46 Pleasant St.
Cambridge, MA 02139   354-8807

WAVAW focuses on educating the community about violence against women such as that depicted in the media, advertising, and pornography. A slide show is available for groups, and WAVAW organizes demonstrations and other actions.

Cape Ann Feminists
P.O. Box 1351
Gloucester, MA 01930   281-3102

Cape Ann Feminists is primarily a networking organization for their area, providing a newsletter to inform local women of activities, women's groups, the Sexual Abuse Hotline, and timely political issues of concern to women.

LUCY STONE
1818–1893

Lucy Stone: "We, the people of the United States. Which 'We, the people'? The women were not included." (New York Tribune, *April, 1853*)

Lucy Stone, a leader in the early struggle for women's rights, came from one of New England's first families. Born in 1818 on a farm near Brookfield, Massachusetts (where her mother had milked eight cows the night before), she was the eighth of nine brothers and sisters.

She learned at a very young age through home, school, and church the inequality of the sexes: Her mother was not allowed to vote, only the boys in the family could go to college, and the Bible said that men should rule women. She saw the injustices of these conditions and devoted her life to changing the status quo.

She supported herself as a teacher until she could afford to pay her way through college. Once there she studied Greek and Hebrew and discovered what she had suspected all long, that the Bible passages regarding women had been translated with gross inaccuracy. She spoke out on the subject whenever she was permitted, but as public speaking was prohibited to women in the 1840s she had few opportunities to do so.

She graduated from Oberlin College in 1847 (the first Massachusetts woman to receive a degree) but refused to write the commencement address because she would not be allowed to read it.

Two years after the Seneca Falls women's rights convention of 1848, she led the first national women's rights convention in Massachusetts. She began traveling and lecturing on woman suffrage and became an eloquent and impressive public speaker in spite of encountering strong male opposition.

When she married Henry Blackwell (brother of two pioneer women physicians, Elizabeth and Emily Blackwell), she not only drew up her own marriage contract but insisted on keeping her own name. Thereafter, a woman who kept her maiden name was called a "Lucy Stoner."

She and her husband eventually settled in Boston, where she became the leading figure in the New England suffrage movement. In 1870 she founded the *Woman's Journal* which was for nearly fifty years the official voice of the National American Woman Suffrage Association.

After her death the journal was edited by her only child, Alice Stone Blackwell.

In Forest Hills Cemetery (95 Forest Hills Avenue, Jamaica Plain) a large copper urn behind an iron grate bears the ashes of Lucy Stone, her husband Henry, and their daughter Alice. A leader even in death, Lucy was the first person in New England to be cremated.

INFORMATION & COMMUNICATIONS

LECTURES

There are approximately thirty institutions of higher learning in the city of Boston itself and well over three hundred in the Greater Boston area. The cultural activities generated by these schools are practically endless. It's safe to say that on almost any given morning, noon, or night there is a lecture going on somewhere in the city.

The Ford Hall Forum (338-5350), the country's oldest continuing public platform, presents free talks by important speakers of the day at the Alumni Hall of Northeastern University. Such outstanding women as Margaret Mead, Eleanor Roosevelt, Ayn Rand, and Angela Davis have spoken before overflow crowds here.

Radcliffe College (495-8000) has any number of lectures going on weekly, such as the Schlesinger Library Luncheon Series (on Notable American Women), the Murray Research Center "brown bag" lunches (women's research), and an evening lecture series at the Cronkite Graduate Center featuring outstanding women writers, poets, and scholars.

Almost all the Boston newspapers, particularly the Thursday edition of the *Globe*, *The Tab*, and the monthly *Sojourner*, contain calendars of these events. Many college newspapers list talks on a wide variety of topics (An Introduction to Islamic Ethics, or Anomalous Quantum Hall Effect, for example) given by well-known professors and speakers. Along with these scholarly events their calendars include art, music, and theater performances and exhibits. These college newspapers can usually be picked up free on campus.

LESSONS

Most of the universities and colleges have extension courses ranging from one-day seminars to full-fledged credit courses. There are also such places as the Boston Center for Adult Education (267-4430) and the Cambridge Center for Adult Education (547-6789) that offer complete catalogues of noncredit courses on everything from Adinkra to Witchcraft.

For complete information on adult-education courses in the Boston area, contact the Educational Exchange of Greater Boston, 430 Mass. Avenue in Cambridge (876-3080). They publish a booklet ($5.95) which lists over seven thousand courses offered by over 255 institutions in the Greater Boston area.

LIBRARIES

It has been said that there are more books than people in Boston — the "Athens of America"; and, in fact, the combined contents of public, academic, and special libraries total well over twelve million volumes. But not only does Boston excel in quantity for the quality of these collections is exceptional, rare, and all-inclusive.

Whether you're a scholar, a researcher, an educator, an artist, or a professional in search of information, there is a library somewhere in Greater Boston to meet your needs.

There's the Countway Library of Medicine at Harvard Medical School with its instant computerized bibliographies, or the Perkins Institute with its famous library for the blind, or Schlesinger Library at Radcliffe College with its outstanding collection of women's history.

The Boston Public Library, founded in 1852, led the way as the first free municipal library in the country and has been the model for most other city libraries. It has over thirty branches, not least of which is the Kirstein Business branch in the heart of the downtown business district, where you have quick access to up-to-the-minute business statistics, directories, and investment information.

The Boston Athenaeum predates even the Boston Public Library by almost fifty years and contains such gems as the personal library of George Washington and a very rare collection of books about Gypsies. The Athenaeum was established as an exclusive men's literary club, and the first woman to break the sex barrier (twenty years after its founding) was Hannah Adams. A pioneering historian, she took her work so seriously and diligently that she was often locked inside the stacks when the librarian went to lunch. She was the first American woman to make a living by writing; and so respected was she by the founders of the Athenaeum that to this day her portrait hangs in the trustees' room.

Another famous Boston author, Lydia Marie Child, was not so lucky, however. She had been welcomed into the Athenaeum as a successful writer of fiction, but when she turned to nonfiction and wrote one of the early antislavery books, the welcome was withdrawn.

All of the universities and colleges in the area have extensive and distinctive libraries. At Harvard, for instance, the Widener Library is considered the largest university library in the world, and there are many separate libraries here such as the Chinese-Japanese Library with the finest collection of Chinese literature this side of the Great Wall.

The Houghton Library at Harvard houses the largest collection of early manuscripts in North America, including the original works of such outstanding women writers as Anne Bradstreet, Emily Dickinson, and Louisa May Alcott. The Dickinson room at the Houghton has a permanent exhibit of Emily's work and is open to visitors Monday to Friday, 9:00 a.m. to 5:00 p.m.

Want to check to see if your ancestors came over on the *Mayflower* or the *Arbella*? The New England Historic Genealogical Society, 101 Newbury Street (536-5740), has the best-known collection of genealogical works in America.

If your ancestors came from Boston, you have the oldest historical society in the country, The Massachusetts Historical Society (536-1608), close at hand for quick research at 1154 Boylston Street. One of their recent exhibits was entitled "Women at Work," and a picture book based on the exhibit is available for purchase at the library. It contains a social history in pictures of American women at work from Colonial times to the early part of this century.

Do you speak French? German? The French Library (266-4351) is at 53 Marlborough and the Goethe Institute (262-6050) at 170 Beacon Street. Both institutions, housed in former Back Bay mansions, offer a variety of cultural activities that are open to the public.

For further information about other special libraries such as the American Jewish Historical Society, the Congregational Library, the Swedenborgian Library, etc., check with the reference librarian at Boston Public Library (536-5400).

PUBLISHING

Alice James Books
138 Mt. Auburn St.
Cambridge, MA 02138   354-1408

Alice James Books is a shared-work cooperative which publishes books of poetry, generally four each year. Primary importance is placed on publishing the work of women. They are committed to giving authors full control over production and management.

Sojourner
143 Albany St.
Cambridge, MA 02139   661-3567

Sojourner is a monthly newspaper/journal for women. Along with local and national news, entertainment and book reviews, and a calendar of women's activities, it also publishes women's poetry and fiction. It has a classified and help-wanted section as well as notices for housing and roommates.

Women's International Network (WIN) News
187 Grant St.
Lexington, MA 02173   862-9431

WIN News is a worldwide open communication system by, for, and about women. It serves the general public, institutions, and organizations by transmitting international information about women and women's groups. The magazine is issued four times a year and is edited by Fran Hoskens.

Luna Press
Box 511, Kenmore Station
Boston, MA 02215   542-9057

Each year Luna Press produces the Lunar Calendar. Beautifully illustrated and designed, "it embraces the real cycles of nature and their effects on individuals and society," according to the editors.

FOCUS

1151 Massachusetts Ave.	616-3633
Cambridge, MA 02138	259-0063

This is the oldest literary journal for lesbians in the country, with over twelve years of continuous publication. They publish bimonthly contributions of poetry, fiction, essays, articles, reviews, graphics, and cartoons, all by women.

WEEA Publishing Center/EDC

55 Chapel St., Suite 208	969-7100
Newton, MA 02160	800-225-3088

The WEEA Publishing Center (whose materials were developed under grants from the US Department of Education, Women's Educational Equity/Act Program) has over two hundred programs and materials specifically developed to promote equity and enhance educational opportunities for girls and women. Career Planning for Minority Women, Women in Jail, Single Mother's Resource Handbook, and Business Management Training for Rural Women are just a few examples of such programs.

The Tab

217 California St.
Newton, MA 02116   969-0340

The Tab is a weekly newspaper with four separate editions (Boston, Cambridge, Brookline, and Newton). Each edition covers news, sports, and entertainment for their localities as well as lengthy classified and calendar sections.

Women in Communications, Inc. (WICI)

1430 Massachusetts Ave., Suite 306–87
Cambridge, MA 02128   482-3663

The Boston Professional Chapter of WICI is an organization for professional women from every area of communications — newspapers, magazines, television, radio, public relations, advertising, film, technical writing, publishing, photojournalism, and communications education. They provide a local and national network, offering

Florence Luscomb, a Boston activist for women's rights, is pictured here in 1912 selling The Woman's Journal *on a Boston street corner.*

support, valuable information, and association with professionals from a variety of fields. They hold their regular chapter meetings on the third Thursday of the month (Sept.–June) at the Copley Plaza in Boston.

Women in Telecommunications
  50 Milk St., 15th Floor
  Boston, MA 02109   451-6505

This is an organization which brings together women in a variety of jobs in the field of telecommunications. They hold monthly meetings that provide a forum for women in this industry.

NEWS IN GENERAL

The following are some of the most popular Boston publications containing local news and calendars of events in and around the city.

Charlotte Cushman, the first great American actress, was born in Boston's North End in 1816.

The Boston Globe

This is Boston's leading daily family newspaper. Confidential Chat is one of the longest-running women's networks in the country. Women with pen names such as "Coupon Sal," "Cold Feet," or "August Tears" have kept up a written correspondence through the Chat pages for years — seeking advice; sharing thoughts, recipes, or adventures; or giving encouragement to others.

The Calendar Section on Thursday has the most extensive listings of current events for the weekend and the coming week. Another special feature in the Thursday edition (as well as in Tuesday's) is the Pulitzer-Prize–winning column of Ellen Goodman.

The Herald

The Herald is Boston's daily tabloid. Lurid headlines, photos of scantily clad women, and sexist ads are among their failings. But instant news, the latest in sports, and several good women reporters on the staff are in their favor. Provocative Norma Nathan keeps a watchful Eye (gossip column) on all the "celebs" in town.

The Boston Phoenix

The *Phoenix* is an avant-garde weekly newspaper with penetrating feature articles on local news. Their weekly listings and reviews of events around town — particularly movies, concerts, and B.A.D. (Boston After Dark) — are exhaustive. Their classified section would have been banned by the old Watch and Ward Society of Boston.

The Christian Science Monitor

The "Monitor" (founded by Mary Baker Eddy) is a nationally distributed daily with high-quality news analysis along with a Boston entertainment section. The works of outstanding local writers and poets often appear in the Home Forum section. Katherine Fanning is the editor.

Boston

A slick monthly magazine with informative local news articles and stories. The On the Town section covers all the current special events of the month.

ABIGAIL ADAMS
1744–1818

*In 1776, Abigail Adams wrote to her husband, John, "I
desire you would remember the ladies and be more generous
and favorable to them than your ancestors."*

Abigail Adams, wife of the second President and mother of the sixth, was a strong and guiding influence on both men throughout her life. Although born in Weymouth and later settling in Quincy, she lived in Boston during one of the country's most important periods of history.

Not far from her front door in Brattle Square (now Court Street), she was to witness and record such historical events as the Boston Massacre and the Boston Tea Party. It was also from this place that in 1774 her husband rode off to Philadelphia as a delegate to the first Continental Congress.

As a result of their long separations she became a prolific letter writer. Always considered by her husband as a full partner and confidante (he referred to her as "the best educated woman I ever met"), she was later to become regarded as one of the nation's first feminists because of her well-known plea to John "to remember the ladies."

In 1776, as the founding fathers set about the task of framing the Constitution, Abigail wrote to John, "By the way in the new code of laws which I suppose it will be necessary for you to make, I desire you would remember the ladies and be more generous and favorable to them than your ancestors! Do not put such unlimited power into the hands of the husbands. Remember all men would be tyrants if they could. If particular care and attention is not paid to the ladies, we are determined to foment a rebellion, and will not be bound by any laws in which we have no voice or representation."

Although John had never before failed to honor his wife's good judgment and thought of her as his equal in all things, he did not take her seriously in this matter.

"As to your extraordinary code of laws, I cannot but laugh," he wrote back. "We have been told that our struggle has loosened the bonds of government everywhere — children and apprentices . . . schools and colleges . . . Indians, Negroes. . . . But your letter was the first intimation that another tribe, more numerous and powerful than all the rest, were grown discontented. . . . We have only the name of masters, and rather than give up this, which would completely subject us to the despotism of the petticoat, I hope General Washington and all our brave heroes would fight!"

Abigail Adams's voluminous correspondence — descriptive, erudite, and full of the spirit of independence — has become an important part of our national historical record. She also planted the seed of liberation that was to flower, only thirty years after her death, at Seneca Falls, New York. It was here, in 1848, that Lucretia Mott and Elizabeth Cady Stanton called together the first women's rights convention to discuss "the social, civil, and religious rights of women."

As Abigail had predicted, the rebellion was beginning to foment.

The Adams National Historic Site on Adams Street and the Abigail Adams House on Franklin Street in Quincy have been scrupulously maintained and are a joy to visit. Abigail's first house remains much as it did when she came to it as a young bride. The bedroom where she bore her son John Quincy Adams in 1767 still has the small, narrow crib, her rope-bed, and her original dressing table.

You can easily reach this site by taking the Red Line from Boston to Quincy Center, which takes less than twenty minutes. The houses are open daily from 9:00 a.m. to 5:00 p.m., April 19 to November 10.

CULTURAL ACTIVITIES

᚜᚜᚜᚜

THE PERFORMING ARTS

Not content to be merely patrons of the arts, Boston women have been actively employed in every major artistic discipline for most of the city's history. Many, in fact, have become world-renowned leaders.

Charlotte Cushman, the first great American actress, was born in Boston's North End and made her first professional appearance in 1835 at the Tremont Theatre. She was affectionately referred to as "our Charlotte" by the national press when she became the first American player of either sex to conquer English audiences.

Jenny Lind, the "Swedish Nightingale" who made $3 million a year at the peak of her career in the mid-1800s, was so successful in Boston that she decided to stay. She married her accompanist at her home in Louisburg Square and formed her own company here.

Nadia Boulanger, famed pianist and music teacher (her list of music students reads like *Who's Who*), became the first woman to conduct the Boston Symphony Orchestra. The first woman to become a member of that orchestra, Doriot Anthony Dwyer, is a descendant of Susan B. Anthony.

Sarah Caldwell founded the now great Opera Company of Boston with only five thousand dollars; and the Elma Lewis School of Fine Arts in Roxbury is the dream of one woman realized.

Folk singer Joan Baez dropped out of Boston University and began writing and singing her folk/protest songs here in Boston and Cambridge during the 1960s. But long before her time, other Boston area women were composing such classics as "The Battle Hymn of the Republic" (Julia Ward Howe) and "America the Beautiful" (Katherine Lee Bates).

Suffice it to say that the talent in this city is endless and the range of cultural activities to showcase it throughout the year is ceaseless. As critic Rebecca West once said, "Most works of art, like most wines, ought to be consumed in the district of their fabrication."

MUSIC

Boston Symphony Orchestra
Symphony Hall
251 Huntington Ave.   266-1492

This is one of the country's finest symphony orchestras, performing from September through April in an equally fine old concert hall. The tickets for many series are generally sold out in advance to long-time subscribers but this doesn't prevent the resourceful person from getting one.

Patrons who cannot attend will phone in their tickets for resale and these go on sale on a first-come-first-serve basis an hour before concert time. Friday matinee tickets are often available around noon on the day of the concert. Also, tickets are sold to rehearsals held Wednesday evenings at 7:30 p.m., where the conductor usually runs through an entire program.

If all else fails, you can hear the concert direct from Symphony Hall over WGBH-FM (Friday) or WCRB-AM and FM (Saturday); and sometimes you can see it as well, via live telecasts by WGBH (Channel 2). Check the local paper for program listings.

Boston Pops Orchestra
Symphony Hall   (C-O-N-C-E-R-T)
251 Huntington Ave.   266-1492

Spring comes to Boston with the May arrival of the Pops. Concert seats are removed and tables and chairs fill the hall. Members of the BSO return; and in a light-hearted fashion (under the direction of

John Williams of *Star Wars* fame) the best-loved musical event in Boston begins.

Blocks of seats are bought out in advance; and while tables on the floor are not readily available, you can usually get balcony seats (often more desirable, as the floor gets noisy) at concert time.

During the summer, free outdoor concerts by the Pops are held at the Hatch Memorial Shell on the Charles River Esplanade. Everyone brings a blanket and a picnic for the two-hour program. And on the Fourth of July, they light up the sky with fireworks.

There are any number of other exceptional musical ensembles playing throughout the year — some of them have been doing so for well over a century. There are also university and foundation series bringing the best musicians in the world to Boston.

You can check the calendar listings in the local paper for information; but for true music lovers, here are a few groups not to be missed: Boston Camerata (262-2092), Boston Philharmonic (536-4001), Boston University Celebrity Series (482-2595), The Cecilia Society (232-4540), Chorus Pro Musica (267-7442), Handel & Haydn Society (266-3605), the New England Conservatory of Music (262-1120, ext. 257), and the Berklee Performance Center (266-7455).

Opera Company of Boston

Opera House
538 Washington St.   426-5300

When Sarah Caldwell started the Opera Company of Boston in 1957, her goal was not only to develop the best opera company in the country but also to keep it from becoming "a crashing bore." And that she did.

Boston audiences have come to expect the unexpected. Clown Emmett Kelly was hired for her production of *The Bartered Bride*; and when Beverly Sills sang her aria in *Daughter of the Regiment*, Caldwell had her slicing potatoes to tempo, assisted by a brandy-toting Saint Bernard.

Her innovative approach to opera has brought rave reviews and international fame. And as might be expected, subscription tickets sell fast. Last-minute tickets (singles particularly) are usually available, but be sure to check the seating plan (see page 101) before purchasing your ticket. That upper balcony is pretty far up.

The Opera Company now has a tradition of performing *Hansel & Gretel* as a special at Christmas time.

There are two other popular opera groups in Boston: Boston Lyric Opera Company at 102 The Fenway (267-1512) and Boston Concert Opera (536-1166) which performs in Jordan Hall. Lyric's *Amahl and the Night Visitors* is another special that has become a Christmas tradition.

BALLET

Boston Ballet Company
553 Tremont St.   542-3945

The Boston Ballet was established in 1965 and since then has built a talented company of fine performers. It also draws upon the services of numerous world-celebrated guest artists. Its presentation of Tchaikovsky's *Nutcracker Suite* has become a Christmas treat for young and old alike.

Tickets for regular performances (February through May at the Wang Center for the Performing Arts) are usually available; but the Christmas show requires advance purchase (although single tickets are often obtainable).

The Wang Center for the Performing Arts (formerly the Metropolitan Center) plays host to a variety of renowned dance troupes and special musical events throughout the year. While the theater has undergone recent renovation, it is cavernous and the acoustics notorious. It seats over four thousand; so anything other than center orchestra, rows A–F in the balcony, or the mezzanine loges will have you craning and straining.

THEATER

While in Boston for a theater engagement in 1869, Mark Twain wrote to his daughter Pamela, "Tomorrow night I appear for the first time before a Boston audience — four thousand critics."

This sentiment still rings true for many performers and playwrights who come to Boston each year with their pre-Broadway shows. It has been estimated that almost a third of all Broadway productions have their tryouts in Boston. Yet many shows, once shown in Boston, never make it to Broadway.

While theatrical enthusiasm is high here, Boston theatergoers are sophisticated and critical — and expect the best. But this hasn't dampened the spirits of the numerous repertory, ethnic, and student groups that continually spring up for a season or two. Often as not, some manage to survive.

The three pre-Broadway theaters (and post-Broadway as well) are the Colonial, the Shubert, and the Wilbur. All three date back to the early part of the century but have undergone, from time to time, extensive renovations. The university theaters, such as the Loeb Drama Center at Harvard, the Huntington at Boston University, and Spingold Arts Center at Brandeis, are among the area's most modern and best equipped stages.

The smaller residential groups convert just about any open space they can find into a stage. While they may not be the most comfortable or prime locations, the talent and enthusiasm usually make up for it.

The Colonial (106 Boylston St., 426-9366), Shubert (265 Tremont St., 426-4520), and Wilbur (246 Tremont St., 423-4008), as mentioned, feature current Broadway hits and tryouts as well as some national touring shows. Orchestra, box seats, and the forward section (rows A–I) of the first balcony in both the Colonial and the Shubert are good seats. Beyond that you have posts and other obstructions to contend with. Second-balcony seats in both theaters require binoculars.

The Wilbur is a smaller theater (twelve hundred seats), and all orchestra and first-balcony seats are very good. The second balcony is also small and the view and sound from here are good too.

The Charles Playhouse (47 Warrenton St., 426-6912) is a small, intimate theater with a three-sided stage. Musicals (with small casts), modern repertories, and new playwrights are often featured here. The first two or three rows in the orchestra put you within spitting distance (literally) of players. Rear orchestra can have you dodging posts. This is one theater where you may prefer the balcony.

Stage II at the Charles Playhouse is cabaret-style and usually lots of fun.

The National Center of Afro-American Artists (Elma Lewis School, 300 Walnut Ave., Roxbury, 442-8820) presents various companies, dance, theater, and music at the center as well as at other locations around the city.

The following resident theaters are very popular with Boston audiences and have been around for some time. Several of them have had award-winning shows which have run for more than a year: Next Move Theatre (1 Boylston Place, 423-5572); Cabaret Theater (275 Tremont St., 423-0912); Lyric Stage (54 Charles St., 742-8703); Little Flags Theatre (location changes, 232-2666); Nucleo Eclettico (216 Hanover St., 367-8056); and Boston Shakespeare Company (300 Massachusetts Ave., 267-5600).

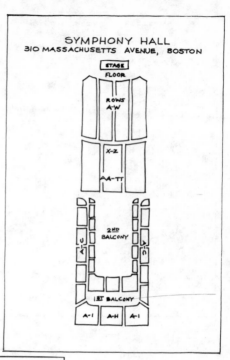

SYMPHONY HALL
310 MASSACHUSETTS AVENUE, BOSTON

STAGE
FLOOR

ROWS
A-W

X-Z

AA-TT

2ND
BALCONY

1ST BALCONY

A-I   A-H   A-I

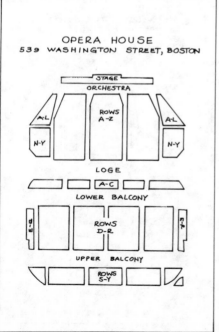

OPERA HOUSE
539 WASHINGTON STREET, BOSTON

STAGE
ORCHESTRA

A-L

ROWS
A-Z

A-L

N-Y

N-Y

LOGE

A-C

LOWER BALCONY

ROWS
D-R

UPPER BALCONY

ROWS
S-Y

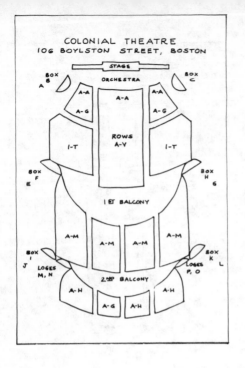

COLONIAL THEATRE
106 BOYLSTON STREET, BOSTON

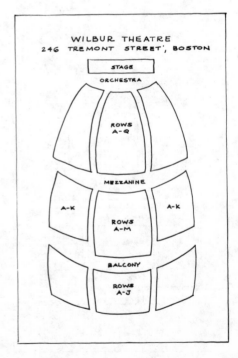

WILBUR THEATRE
246 TREMONT STREET, BOSTON

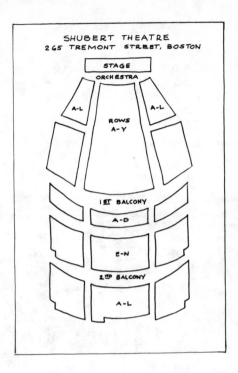

SHUBERT THEATRE
265 TREMONT STREET, BOSTON

STAGE

ORCHESTRA

A-L

A-L

ROWS
A-Y

1 ST BALCONY

A-D

E-N

2 nd BALCONY

A-L

The university theaters are: American Repertory Theatre (Loeb Drama Center, 64 Brattle St., Cambridge, 547-8300); The Huntington Theatre Company (Boston University, 264 Huntington Ave., 266-3996); Spingold Theatre (Brandeis University, Waltham, 894-4343); and Tufts Arena Theater (Medford, 381-3493).

Tickets to all major theaters should be bought in advance to insure availability and good seats. They can be purchased at the box office, or by phone if you have a major credit card. Tickets to these shows are expensive but there are a few exceptions.

Pre-Broadway shows generally have two or three preview performances at reduced prices. Also, at BOSTIX in Faneuil Hall Marketplace tickets are sold at half price for same-day performances. There is no guarantee that the show you waited (almost always) in line for will be available — but you are sure to get something worthwhile.

BOSTIX (723-5181) also handles discount coupon books for a nominal fee for tourist attractions, museums, historical sights, and films. You can also purchase advance-sale tickets at full price to all theatrical events. They accept cash only (no refunds or exchanges) and are open

Monday through Saturday 11:00 a.m. to 6:00 p.m., Sunday 12:00 to 6:00. (Closed Thanksgiving, Christmas, and New Year's Day.)

Regular ticket agencies that charge a slight commission are Elsie's (424-1300), Hub (426-8340), Tyson (426-2662), and Out of Town in Cambridge (492-1900).

Do keep in mind that the theater district is unfortunately (as in New York City) located in the sleaziest part of town. It borders the Combat

Elma Lewis, founder and director of the well-known Elma Lewis School of Fine Arts, has provided educational and cultural opportunities for hundreds of Boston's young people.

Zone with its strip joints, porno book shops, and greasy spoons. While some police say that crime is actually low here, it's not a pleasant place to walk around in.

If you are staying in one of the nearby hotels, such as the Park Plaza or the 57 Park Plaza, it is reasonably safe to walk to and from the theater. Taxis are readily available in front of either of these hotels if you have farther to go.

MOVIES

Boston ranks as one of the top three cities in the country in the American art-film market. There are a number of first-run art houses here; most notable are the Nickelodeon (424-1500), the Exeter Street Theatre (536-7067), the Orson Welles (868-3600), and the Coolidge Corner (734-2500).

Brattle Theatre (876-4226) and Harvard Square Theatre (864-4580), as well as some of the art museums and colleges, continually show vintage classics. The Galeria Cinema (661-3737) just off Harvard Square not only has good movies but is one of the few theaters around where your shoes don't stick to the floor.

The Sack chain recently opened a new nine-screen theater in Copley Plaza and features first-run movies as well as revivals. You can purchase your ticket in the morning for an evening performance if you like.

The Cheri Complex (three screens) is opposite the Sheraton Boston Hotel and next door to the Hilton; the 57 Cinema is next to the 57 Park Plaza and across from the Boston Park Plaza Hotel; and the Sack Charles is next to the Holiday Inn at Government Center. All of these theaters show first-run movies, and you will find a listing of their current offerings in the local papers.

If you like cartoons you can enjoy them cabaret-style at Off the Wall on Pearl Street in Central Square (547-5255).

MUSEUMS

Gardner Museum

The museums of Boston are, by and large, an outstanding lot, but none is quite so extraordinary as the Isabella Stewart Gardner Museum in the Boston Fens. What makes this one so exceptional is its creator, the legendary "Mrs. Jack" herself — Isabella Stewart Gardner.

She was one of the most exciting and colorful women to brighten the somber Victorian scene in Boston during the mid-nineteenth century. Although born in New York and educated abroad, she moved to Boston in 1860 when she married one of the town's wealthiest and most eligible bachelors, John Lowell Gardner.

But like many newcomers to Boston society before her, Isabella was snubbed as an outsider by the proper Brahmins. A brilliant and spirited young woman, she retaliated by becoming just about as improper as she dared.

Her antics soon became legend. She walked down Tremont Street with a lion named Rex on a leash. On shopping trips around Boston she never left her carriage but insisted that salesmen accommodate her with curb service. Instead of drinking tea she drank beer.

She poked fun at the many exclusive Boston clubs by forming her own and calling it the "It" club. While other Boston women kept their jewels locked away, she wore two huge diamonds set on gold wire springs tucked into her hair and they fluttered above her head like butterfly antennae. On occasion she greeted guests to her Beacon Street home from the bottom branch of a mimosa tree.

John Singer Sargent painted her portrait, and even that created a scandal. She posed in a black, low-necked gown with a rope of pearls around her waist and a black shawl drawn about her hips to accentuate her figure. When the portrait was exhibited it generated so many hostile comments that Mr. Gardner declared he would never exhibit it again.

Mrs. Jack, as she was called (behind her back), became through the years a connoisseur of fine art and antiques and acquired a large collection during her many travels abroad. When her husband died, she decided to build a palace to house her treasures. She constructed a magnificent Venetian palazzo on newly filled Boston fenland that had previously been a dump site.

The grand opening of her Fenway Court was held on a cold, wintry New Year's Day in 1903. To the strains of music played by the Boston Symphony Orchestra the dazzled guests were greeted by cascading masses of fragrant flowers, flickering candles from the multitiered balconies, and a flower-bedecked, glistening fountain in the center of a large indoor courtyard.

To this day, whenever you enter Fenway Court you will be greeted by similar masses of exquisite, fragrant flowers surrounding the central courtyard with its splashing fountain.

Besides Italian architecture with Chinese and Spanish influences in many of the rooms, you will find a rich collection of paintings by Raphael, Rembrandt, and Rubens as well as such nineteenth-century artists as Sargent, Manet, Degas, and Whistler. And of course the famous portrait of Mrs. Jack, by Sargent, is now permanently on display.

Isabella Stewart Gardner as she was "scandalously" painted by John Singer Sargent in 1888.

Everything has been kept exactly as she left it, and her will states that nothing must ever be changed.

The museum is open Tuesday noon until 9:00 p.m. (July and August till 5:00 p.m.) and Wednesday through Sunday until 5:00 p.m., but closed on Mondays. There are concerts September through June every Thursday at noon, Sunday at 3:00 p.m., and Tuesday at 6:00 p.m. in the Tapestry Room. There is a small cafe with an outdoor terrace (summer only). You can reach the museum (734-1359) by taking an Arborway car on the Green Line.

The Museum of Fine Arts

The Museum of Fine Arts ranks among the most important art museums in the world. It is the second largest comprehensive art museum in this country (the Metropolitan in New York is greater). It is one of the few museums in the world that is entirely supported by private contributions (as opposed to government funding).

Just about every taste in art can be satisifed here, from interests in ancient Minoan civilization to twentieth-century American paintings. There are period rooms completely reconstructed, such as a fifteenth-century Tudor room from England, an eighteenth-century Louis XVI salon from France, and a seventeenth-century early-American kitchen from Massachusetts.

The Museum's collection of paintings has examples of all the important schools of Europe and America, particularly French impressionists and Colonial American portraits (some still showing musket holes created by British fire). The old masters are well represented by Rubens, Rembrandt, van Dyck, El Greco, Titian and Tintoretto.

The Oriental galleries and the Egyptian collections are both extensive and exceptional. The museum also has one of the most outstanding textile collections in the world. Special exhibits are held from time to time; but several of the period rooms have fine examples of needlework chair seats, embroidered fireplace screens, crewel bed coverings, and needlework pictures continually on display.

Beautiful examples of sculpture are scattered throughout the museum, including Frederich MacMonnies's "Bacchante." This statue was originally intended for the Boston Public Library but the prim trustees were shocked by her nudity and what they called "her effusive, gleeful drunkenness" and what was perceived as "her irresponsibility as a mother." The MFA gladly received it when the library refused it and displays it proudly just to the left of the lower rotunda.

The museum is open Tuesday through Sunday 10:00 a.m. to 5:00 p.m. (Wednesday until 10:00 p.m.), and is closed on Monday. There are a cafeteria, a cafe, a restaurant, and a well-stocked museum gift and book shop. Admission is $3.50 but there are free introductory guided tours. For recorded listings of weekly events simply dial A-N-S-W-E-R-S. The museum can be reached by the Arborway E car on the Green Line.

Boston's Museum of Science

This is definitely a hands-on museum for those who like to get involved and discover the wonders of science. See life begin in the chicken hatchery, hear your voice on the telephone or see your picture on television. Hear the transparent woman discuss her anatomy or play tic-tac-toe with a computer. Make your hair stand on end, or test your brain's reactions. For a tour of distant galaxies or to watch the seasonal starlit skies over Boston, visit the Hayden Planetarium. These are just a few of the endless experiences you can indulge in at the Museum of Science.

In general the Museum is open from 9:00 to 4:00 and up to 10:00 p.m. on Friday night. On Sunday it opens at 10:00 a.m. and closes at 5:00 p.m. The holiday schedule is erractic so it is best to call 742-6088 for recorded information. The Skyline Cafeteria, which overlooks the Charles River, is open every day for lunch and on Friday nights for dinner. Admission is $2.75 for children and $4.50 for adults, with an additional charge of 50 cents for the Planetarium. You can reach the museum on the Lechmere branch of the Green Line.

Fogg Art Museum

The Museum was endowed by Mrs. Elizabeth Fogg in 1895 in memory of her husband. As a teaching museum for Harvard University it houses one of the most extensive art collections of any university in the world. On permanent display are Oriental and classical works of art, a collection of English silver, late-medieval Italian painting, French Romanesque sculpture, French impressionists, and postimpressionist drawings, painting, and sculpture.

The museum is open Monday through Friday from 9:00 a.m. to 5:00 p.m., Saturday 10:00 a.m. to 5:00 p.m., and Sunday 2:00 p.m. to 5:00 p.m. (closed Saturday and Sunday, July and August). Admission is free and you can reach the museum (32 Quincy Street, Cambridge, 495-7768) on the Red Line to Harvard Square.

The Botanical Museum of Harvard University

This is another Harvard museum that owes its success to the generosity of women benefactors. Mrs. Elizabeth C. Ware and her daughter Miss Mary Lee Ware of Boston donated the famous "garden in glass" to the university as a gift in memory of Dr. Charles Eliot Ware.

The Ware Collection at the Botanical Museum is better known as the world-famous "glass flowers." Originally intended as a tool to teach the students botany in the late 1800s, this is an exhibit of over seven hundred plant species magnificently crafted by two German artists, Leopold Blaschka and his son Rudolf. Scientists have marveled at the artistic skill that created such accuracy and beauty. This is Harvard's most popular public attraction and thousands of visitors come here each year specifically to see the "glass flowers."

The museum (which also houses Harvard's other science museums) is open Monday through Saturday 9:00 a.m. to 4:30 p.m., and Sunday 1:00 p.m. to 4:30 p.m. The admission charge of $1.50 covers all Harvard science museums, and they can be reached by the Red Line to Harvard Square and a short walk through Harvard Yard to 24 Oxford Street. For further information call 495-3045.

The Busch-Reisinger Museum

The Busch-Reisinger Museum at Harvard University was founded in 1902 for the study of Germanic culture and now is considered to have one of the most important and extensive collections of Central and Northern European art outside of Europe. It has a distinguished collection of twentieth-century German works, most notably from the Bauhaus school. Concerts are given occasionally on the internationally famous Flentrop organ and there is a small outdoor sculpture garden with lunch tables for picnicking. The museum (free) is open Monday through Saturday 9:00 a.m. to 4:45 p.m.; closed major holidays and Sundays, and Saturday during July and August. The museum can be reached by the Red Line to Harvard Square and a short walk to 29 Kirkland Street (495-2317).

Boston Children's Museum

The Children's Museum began in 1913 and moved to its present location on the waterfront in 1979. *People* magazine calls it "The country's best museum for kids" — and they definitely mean "kids" of all ages. It's also one of the best resource centers for anyone involved with children's education.

Imaginative exhibits and challenging experiments allow everyone to get into the act. A large Resource Center contains a library, learning materials, study kits, activity kits, and curriculum units to be used in schools.

An innovative and popular spot is the Recycle Store which contains barrels of inexpensive materials discarded by factories that are ideal for science, art, and craft projects. You can fill a bag for $1.00 and buy a copy of *Recyclopedia* in the museum bookstore to find easy directions for projects. The museum (426-8855) is open Tuesday–Sunday, 10:00 a.m. to 5:00 p.m.; Friday until 9:00 p.m. It is open on Mondays during the summer and on school holidays. The museum can be reached by the Red Line to South Station and a short walk down Congress Street to Museum Wharf.

Institute of Contemporary Art (ICA)

The ICA, housed in a cleverly renovated fire station, exhibits contemporary art by local, national, and international artists in a variety of media and a wide diversity of styles.

A cross-section of some of the most significant art and artists of the day are displayed here in paintings, drawings, prints, sculpture, architecture, photography, video, film, dance, literature, and music.

A full schedule of activities goes on throughout the year including informal discussions, a lecture series, poetry and film programs, and guided tours. The museum is open Tuesday through Saturday 11:00 a.m. to 7:00 p.m. (closed on Monday). There is an admission charge of $2.50 (free on Wednesday) and an Arts/Information line, 266-5151. The museum is at 955 Boylston Street, across from Hynes Auditorium, and can be reached at the Auditorium stop on the Green Line.

Several smaller museums in the area are worthy of note. Many of them are open daily; others are open for special events. It's best to call ahead for current hours and exhibit information.

Bunker Hill Museum, 241-8220

John F. Kennedy Library & Museum, 929-4567

Margaret Compton Gallery (MIT), 253-4444

Museum of Afro-American History, 445-7400

Museum of the American China Trade, 696-1815

ART GALLERIES

Art galleries such as the Vose have been exhibiting their treasures on Newbury Street since the mid-1800s. So populated is this street with galleries that twice a year the gallery owners band together and close the street to vehicular traffic. Musicians perform outside and artists paint on the street, while all the galleries remain open for the day.

Many of the galleries feature the works of local artists while other specialize in eighteenth- and nineteenth-century American and European painters. The Copley Society of Boston (158 Newbury) and The Guild of Boston Artists (162) both promote and support the work of gifted artists from this area.

Judi Rotenberg, born and educated in Boston, exemplifies the talent that abounds here. Her own gallery at 130 Newbury is ablaze with her vibrant watercolors of Boston scenes. Her works have been highlighted at Paris art exhibits and she was recently honored by the Society of French Independent Artists.

Other Newbury Street galleries emphasizing contemporary art are the Harcus Gallery (7 Newbury), Barbara Krakow (10), Helen Shlien (14), Alpha (121) Pucker/Safrai (171–173), and Thomas Segal (73).

Those featuring early American and European paintings, prints, and drawings are Childs (169), English Gallery (212), and Tom Renn Gallery (20).

The Fort Point Channel area, down toward the harbor on Congress Street, is the newest site for several galleries. Bromfield Gallery at 354 Congress Street (426-8270) is an organization of over nine hundred professional artists whose works share exhibit space in this converted nineteenth-century building. The Lopoukhine Gallery (426-4973) is also located here.

Lower Tremont Street is yet another popular area for local artists, with the Mills Gallery at the Boston Center for the Arts (549 Tremont) and the Gallery at the Piano Factory (791 Tremont).

Most of the galleries on Newbury Street are open Monday through Saturday from 9:00 to 5:00. A few are closed on Monday, and quite a few are closed during July and August. The Fort Point Channel and Tremont Street galleries tend to open later in the morning and on fewer days, so phone ahead before you go.

THINGS TO DO

rrrrr

SIGHTSEEING

THE WOMEN'S FREEDOM TRAIL

When it comes to national historic treasures, Boston's Freedom Trail ranks right up there with the White House, the Statue of Liberty, and the Golden Gate Bridge. In fact, to the thousands of descendants claiming lineage back to the *Mayflower* and the *Arbella*, it does indeed top them all. It is one of the most popular tourist attractions in Boston.

The Freedom Trail is a walking tour covering some important historical sites and structures that figured prominently in Colonial and Revolutionary times.

Carefully laid out in red bricks and painted lines, the Freedom Trail leads you from site to site much like Dorothy's yellow-brick road. As it is dominated by churches, meeting houses, graveyards, and battle scenes, it may also sound as depressing, if not as hazardous, as that fabled road to Oz ("Lions and tigers and bears, Oh my!").

For our purposes, however, it does wind through several interesting streets formerly populated by some of Boston's most outstanding founding mothers. And while it does not end at the Wizard's palace, you'll definitely be the wiser for having traveled it.

Most of the historic buildings (State House, Faneuil Hall, and the Revere House) have restroom facilities. Just opposite the Old State House is the National Park Visitor Center which also has restrooms. Here you can obtain information on all the activities going on in Boston, locations of all the National Parks, as well as maps and brochures on most historical sites in the area. The guides here are friendly and helpful and will answer any questions, give directions, and offer some suggestions.

Whole books have been written about the Freedom Trail, and if you're a real history buff you'll find armfuls of reading material along the way describing each landmark in exhausting detail.

But for those of you who are already beginning to yawn we offer this cursory view — an instant mini-course — on some of Boston's historical sights. We've paid special attention to one aspect that the official guidebooks have a tendency to overlook, if not ignore. And that, of course, is the part that women, the founding mothers, have contributed along the way to freedom.

Boston Common

The usual place to begin is on the Boston Common at the Visitor Information Center, which can easily be reached by the Green or the Red Line, exiting at Park Street station. If you are coming by car, there is an underground parking garage on Charles Street (beneath the Common).

The Boston Common encompasses forty-eight acres set aside in 1634 as a "trayning field" for the militia and a grazing ground for "cattell." It soon, however, became the site of the pillory where husbands were put into stocks for kissing their wives in public, where "nagging" wives were punished in the ducking stool, and where several women were hanged as witches or Quakers.

Although the Puritans fled to this country in search of religious freedom, their tolerance did not extend to Quakers. The Quakers believed in such odd things as sexual equality, high standards of education for female children, and legitimacy for women preachers. To the Puritans this was heresy. They believed in a strict code of ethical and moral behavior, while the Quakers placed the greatest emphasis on the primacy of individual conscience. Thus, Quakers found themselves unwelcomed in Boston.

Statue of Mary Dyer in front of the East Wing of the Massachusetts State House, Beacon Hill, Boston.

In spite of this, two Quaker women, Mary Fisher and Ann Austin, attempted to come to Boston in 1656. According to Judge Samuel Sewall, who wrote in his diary at the time, "They were stript naked under pretence to know whether they were witches, tho' in searching, no token was found upon them but of innocense. And in the search they were so barbarously misused that modesty forbids to mention it." The women were banished from the Commonwealth under penalty of death if they returned.

Another Quaker woman, however, determined to defy the "wicked law" against her religion, returned to Boston after being banished. Her name was Mary Dyer and in 1660 she was hanged on the Common as "a flag for others to take example by."

Now, more than three centuries after her death, a poignant statue of Mary Dyer by Quaker Sylvia Shaw Judson has been placed on the State House grounds, showing for all to see the "witness for religious freedom." The inscription on the base of the statue quotes the martyred woman: "My life not availeth me in comparison to the liberty of the truth."

Over the years, the Common increasingly became a forum for public debate; it remains so today. Many well-known women have stood on hastily erected platforms here, expounding on a variety of social and civic causes.

In 1851, Amelia Bloomer, temperance reformer, suffragist, and editor, came to Boston to speak out on women's rights. As she stepped up on a park bench in the Common to make her appeal, she was booed down and whistled at by men in the audience because of the costume she was wearing.

She had recently adopted "panteletts," which had been introduced into this country by the famous English actress, Fanny Kemble. Women were quickly adopting this costume as a sensible alternative to the tight corsets and heavy petticoats that helped to keep them "in their place."

A Boston editor, writing about the incident in the park, dubbed Amelia's costume "Bloomers" and anyone who wore them a "Bloomer Girl." The title stuck, and while in defiance (as well as comfort) Amelia continued to wear the costume for several years, eventually she gave it up because she felt it was distracting attention from the more important issues in the struggle for women's rights.

Crossing over Tremont Street by the Information Center, you will come to West Street. Elizabeth Peabody lived at number 13 (now demolished), where she opened a book shop in her home — an unheard-of thing for a woman to do in 1840.

It was soon to become the most influential bookstore in Boston, eventually leading the proprietor into the publishing business. As the first woman publisher not only in Boston but in the whole country, Elizabeth published the works of many prominent authors, including Thoreau's *Civil Disobedience*.

It was also here that the feminist writer Margaret Fuller held her famous Conversations for women on Wednesday evenings.

The State House

The State House, with its golden dome and Bulfinch front, stands on the highest point in the city, Beacon Hill. Built in 1795 and replete with statues and portraits of the founding fathers, it remained for years a bastion of male supremacy.

Then in 1838, Angelina Grimké, the most eloquent abolitionist speaker of the day, was invited to address the Great and General Court on the subject of abolition of slavery. This created an uproar among some of the legislators. Not only was it frowned upon for women to speak before a mixed audience of men and women, but to have it take place in this venerated chamber bordered on blasphemy.

In spite of a barrage of hooting and howling from some of the men at the beginning of her speech, by the time she had finished she had won their fervent support for her petition.

Along with her sister Sarah, who joined her in the fight for equality, she continued to speak out and write on the subject. In 1839 the two sisters compiled from reports, newspaper clippings, and letters, a document entitled *American Slavery As It Is: Testimony of a Thousand Witnesses*. It was this document that Harriet Beecher Stowe was to draw upon for her material for *Uncle Tom's Cabin*.

Angelina Grimké was among the first abolitionists to see the connection between the fight for black freedom and the rights of women, and she continued the struggle for woman suffrage long after the passage of the Fourteenth and Fifteenth Amendments.

Although born in South Carolina, the sisters eventually settled in the Hyde Park section of Boston. Both of them are buried in the Mount Hope Cemetery in Dorchester.

In 1843 another woman and great reformer, Dorothea Dix, was to address the Massachusetts legislature; and this time there was less fanfare. In an impassioned plea, she exposed the inhumane treatment of the insane in the city jail. The Court responded to her report by adopting the Massachusetts Hospital Bill, laying the foundation for proper treatment for the mentally ill and, eventually, for prison reform.

Continuing her crusade for better facilities for prisoners and the mentally ill, Dix traveled throughout the country visiting prisons and speaking before other state legislators, converting them to the cause. Through her efforts, over 119 asylums and hospitals were built in the next few years, and public attitude toward the mentally ill began to improve.

These two women, Grimké and Dix, led the way for countless other women who have long since come forth from their once segregated seats in the balcony to take their rightful places on the platform of the Great and General Court.

While we have not yet elected a woman to fill the top seat in Massachusetts's government, that of governor, the day is close at hand. Presently there are four women serving on the governor's eleven-person cabinet; and one of the top jobs in the nation's capital, secretary of the Department of Health and Human Services, is held by the former congresswoman from Massachusetts, Margaret Heckler.

ANGELINA GRIMKÉ
1805–1879

The first woman to address a United States legislative body,
in the Senate Chamber in the Massachusetts State House,
February 21, 1838.

"I stand before you as a moral being, endowed with precious and unalienable rights, which are correlative with solemn duties and high responsibilities; and as a moral being I feel that I owe it to the suffering slave, and to the deluded master, to my country and my world, to do all that I can to overturn a system of complicated crimes, built up upon the broken hearts and prostrate bodies of my countrymen in chains, and cemented by the blood and sweat and tears of my sisters in bonds."

Although the increased presence of women in the State House is apparent on a physical level, it is only minimally reflected in the plethora of artwork in these hallowed halls. Anne Hutchinson and Mary Dyer, whose two imposing statues flank the entrances to the East and West Wings of the State House, are the only women so honored.

It is significant, however, that the statue standing between these two martyrs, on the front lawn of the State House, is that of Horace Mann who declared in 1850 that female education "must be rescued from its present reproach of inferiority, and advanced to an equality with that of males."

The graceful bronze of Mann was sculpted by Emma Stebbins and erected in 1865. It was a gift from the schoolchildren and teachers of the state in recognition of Mann's service in developing and improving the system of popular education in Massachusetts.

In the south entrance to the Senate Staircase Hall is another beautiful bronze statue, this one done by Bella L. Pratt (who also did the two flanking the front entrance to the Boston Public Library). It is a memorial dedicated to the army nurses of the Civil War and was placed in the hall in 1914.

In accepting the statue at its unveiling, Governor David I. Walsh said, "I accept it in the name of all people of Massachusetts . . . to remind a careless world . . . that she who heals the wounds of valor and allays the anguish of glory is as worthy of honor and remembrance as the great captain whose genius has annihilated armies and saved nations."

The State House is open Monday to Friday from 9:00 a.m. to 5:00 p.m. and there are guided tours by the "Doric Dames" from 10:00 to 4:00.

Just down Beacon Street from the State House is an alleyway called Tremont Place. During the 1870s and the 1880s, number 3 was the headquarters of the Massachusetts Woman Suffrage Association. It was here that such women as Julia Ward Howe, Lucy Stone, and Alice Stone Blackwell worked to attain the right for women to vote.

Boston women did secure, through their efforts, the right to vote in school board elections in 1879, and by 1893 the right to vote in municipal elections. It wasn't until 1920, however, that their long-sought-after goal, the right to vote in national elections, was realized.

Park Street Church

Park Street Church, located on the corner of Park and Tremont Streets (also called "Brimstone Corner" for the fiery sermons once emanating from here), has a long history and is the site of many firsts.

The first attack against slavery was preached here in 1829 by William Lloyd Garrison; in 1831 "America" was sung and heard here for the first time; the American Temperance Society was founded here in

1826; and Mary Baker Eddy held one of her first Boston meetings in an adjoining building.

Also, during a period of decline in the late 1800s, this was the first church to rent out its lower level for commercial purposes — a tearoom. The tearoom, however, was short-lived; its lease was quickly canceled when it was discovered that the management allowed women to smoke on the premises. The church is open from 9:30 until 4:00, Tuesday through Saturday during July and August only.

Just behind the Park Street Church, at number 4 Park Street, was the home of *The Women's Journal*. This paper, which had many distinguished editors and contributors, was the voice of the American Woman Suffrage Association from 1870 to 1917.

Granary Burying Ground

The Old Granary Burying Ground next to the Park Street Church takes its name from a storage barn that once stood on this site. The Granary was part of the early colonists' first welfare program. The intent was to store surplus corn and wheat here, and then, in times of scarcity, sell it at a low cost to those in need.

The project was short-lived, however, as the Colonial mice became the constant beneficiaries. The name was all that was left; and thus the leading patriots of the day — governors, ministers, and some of the signers of the Declaration of Independence — were buried here in the Old Granary.

Many husbands and wives are buried together here, but the largest and most impressive memorial stone is that of Abiah and Josiah Franklin. It has a long inscription ending with "He was a pious and prudent man; She a discreet and virtuous woman."

The Franklins lived not far from this site, on Milk Street, where Mrs. Franklin gave birth to seventeen children (only thirteen survived). The fifteenth child, whom she named Benjamin, and who grew up to become an American statesman, is often called "Boston's favorite son." Abiah has never been given the distinction of being called "Boston's favorite mother."

One of the most sought-out graves here, though, is that of "Mother Goose," where Elizabeth Foster Vergoose was buried (see page 122).

The cemetery is open every day from 8:00 a.m. to 4:00 p.m.

MOTHER GOOSE

N o one knows for sure who the real Mother Goose is, but many American scholars are of the opinion that she was a kindly grandmother who lived on Pudding Lane (now Devonshire Street) in Boston. After all, she's buried in the Old Granary Burying Ground on Beacon Hill.

In 1690, at the age of twenty-seven, Elizabeth Foster married Isaac Goose (originally Vergoose), who had ten children, and then proceeded to have six of her own. Unlike the old women who lived in a shoe, Mother Goose knew just what to do with her many children — she entertained them with songs and ditties that she made up.

Years later she went to live with her daughter and son-in-law and continued to delight her grandchildren with her repertoire. Her son-in-law, a prosperous printer by the name of Thomas Fleet, was so charmed by this collection of nonsense that he decided to put the rhymes into print. They were made into a book called *Songs for the Nursery or Mother Goose's Melodies*.

Unfortunately, no copy of Thomas Fleet's original American Mother Goose collection is now known to exist. So if you love to browse in old bookstores or flea markets, here's one more treasure to keep an eye out for. It would be worth a small fortune if you could find one.

King's Chapel

King's Chapel was organized in 1686 as the first Church of England. Inside you will see the large canopied pew where royal governors worshipped, and where President Washington sat in 1789. The pew was dismantled in 1826 as "an undemocratic reminder of another era" but was rebuilt a century later.

The walls and chancel are rimmed with busts of ministers and other notable male members of the congregation, but little evidence can be seen that women ever worshipped here. The "annals" (several volumes of historical records) reveal, however, the unsung heroines who have maintained and supported the church over the centuries.

In writing the third volume of the annals, the Reverend John C. Perkins notes that although King's Chapel women have never been elected to the vestry, there are "few elements of church life which have not been profoundly influenced" by them.

He tells a particularly poignant story of Miss Sarah Elizabeth Manning, "a frail little woman" who began appearing at the church in the early 1900s. There was a "quaintness and Dickensian quality" to her, according to Perkins, and she "looked like someone in need."

She lived alone in a small room behind the State House and had no friends or relatives, but "few storms could keep her from Sunday morning services," he notes.

One day her landlady sent word to the church that Miss Manning was ill, and when some church members arrived she requested help in drawing up a will. The church members cast their eyes over the meager surroundings but benevolently catered to the dying woman's wish and brought her pencil and paper.

She died a few days later, leaving all her worldly goods to the church. Quite to everyone's surprise she was in possession of several bank books totaling over $35,000 — the largest single gift ever made to King's Chapel up to that time.

The beautiful marble chancel floor was built as a gift from Mary Bartlett in memory of her sister, Fannie Bartlett. Fannie, according to the annals, "made a life-work of the establishment of the Instructive District Nursing Association — one of the most beneficent charities ever set up in Boston."

The Bartlett sisters have the distinction of being the only two women to have their names engraved within this sanctuary.

The chapel is open Tuesday through Saturday from 10:00 a.m. to 4:00 p.m. Church services are held on Sunday at 11:00 a.m. and Wednesday at 12:15 p.m. (September through June).

King's Chapel Burying Ground

Established in 1630, this is the oldest cemetery in the city. Among the early colonists buried here is Mary Chilton, the first woman to set foot on New England soil. Not far from Mary Chilton's grave is that of Elizabeth Pain.

Nathaniel Hawthorne's classic novel, *The Scarlet Letter*, written in 1850, was based on the life of Elizabeth Pain. She had a child born out of wedlock, fathered by her minister, and for this "crime" was made to wear a large scarlet letter A, for adulteress, on the bodice of her clothes.

This is an interesting place to wander around reading epitaphs. You will notice that quite often the gravestones will read: "Martha Winthrop, relict of . . ."; relict being an archaic term for "widow." One of our favorites is, "Here lies interred the remains of Mrs. Elizabeth Foster, comfort of Mr. Elisha Foster."

Old Corner Book Store

The northwest corner of Washington and School streets is the site of the first women's club in America. Here, in her home, Anne Hutchinson instituted weekly gatherings of women to discuss the sermons of the Reverend John Cotton. The Hutchinson homestead is no longer standing, but the present building dates back to 1712 and has been a bookstore since 1828.

In the later part of the nineteenth century, this site once again became a famous meeting place. This time it was the leading authors of the day who met here — Julia Ward Howe, Harriet Beecher Stowe, and a few famous gentlemen, such as Hawthorne, Longfellow, and Emerson.

The proprietor of the shop, James T. Fields, who was also their publisher, encouraged his authors to gather here for lively discussions and conversations. Annie Fields, his wife, entertained them in her home on Charles Street as well and was instrumental in bringing together such luminaries as Willa Cather and Sarah Orne Jewett.

Mrs. Field eventually published several books of her own, chief among them three volumes of poetry and various works of literary reminiscence of those early days. The latter included her voluminous correspondence with Harriet Beecher Stowe, Sarah Orne Jewett, and Celia Thaxter.

The building was rescued from certain demolition in the early 1960s by a group of civic-minded citizens and restored to its original charm. The *Boston Globe* now has an office here but the building remains, for

ANNE HUTCHINSON
1591–1643

"A courageous exponent of civil liberty and religious toleration." (Inscription on statue of Anne Hutchinson in front of West Wing of the Massachusetts State House.)

Anne Hutchinson came to Boston with her husband in 1634, soon after the colony had been established. As a nurse, a midwife, and "a woman of piety, ready talent and flow of speech," she gained instant popularity and stature in the community.

In response to the sermons of the Reverend John Cotton, with whom she disagreed, she began to hold meetings in her home each week to review and discuss his sermons. In the beginning, these gatherings were chiefly attended by women, but soon they were attracting the interest of such men as the young governor, Sir Harry Vane.

Her critical comments against Cotton's doctrine of "the covenant of work" as opposed to her own espousal of the "covenant of grace" (believing that faith alone was necessary for salvation) eventually drew disfavor from the religious hierarchy.

She was brought before the General Court, and although pregnant and ill, courageously defended herself and her followers. Refusing the court's decision to grant her a pardon if she would wholly and ignominiously retract her statements, she and her followers were banished from Massachusetts as being "unfit for a good society."

With her family and friends she moved to Rhode Island, where she helped to found the town of Portsmouth. When her husband died, and fearing that the jurisdiction of Massachusetts might be extended to Rhode Island, she took her younger children to a new settlement on Long Island Sound. Soon after arriving there, however, she and all but her youngest child were massacred by a band of Siwanoy Indians.

It took over three hundred years for her to live down the words of John Winthrop, the first governor of Massachusetts, who characterized her as "a goodly woman and of special parts, who had lost her understanding by occasion of her giving herself wholly to reading and writing; whereas, if

she had attended to her household affairs and such things as belong to women, and had not gone out of her way and calling to meddle in such things as are proper for men, whose minds are stronger, she had kept her wits and might have improved them usefully and honorably in the place of God set her."

The bronze statue in front of the West Wing of the State House represents Anne with her small daughter by her side. It was given to the Commonwealth in 1922 by the Anne Hutchinson Memorial Association and the State Federation of Women's Clubs in honor of "a courageous exponent of civil liberty and religious toleration."

It wasn't until 1945, however, that the Great and General Court of Massachusetts formally revoked the edict of banishment against her.

---

the most part, a bookstore — the Globe Corner Bookstore. Many new and old books on New England can be purchased here.

There are several display cases containing first editions of books from earlier days; and one in particular was the "most sensational" book ever to be sold in the store. The book, *Cape Cod Folks*, published in 1881, turned out to be a modified *Peyton Place* of its day.

It seems that the author, Sally Pratt McLean, wrote an amusing story based on her experiences as a schoolteacher in Cedarville (part of Plymouth). The trouble was that, unbeknown to the publisher, she gave all the characters in her book the names of persons actually living in Cedarville.

The publisher tried to recall the books when he found this out, but it was too late. Irate townspeople threatened lawsuits, claiming they had been ridiculed; even when the publisher turned out the second edition with names changed the townspeople were not appeased.

As for Ms. McLean, she had a best seller for several years.

The Globe Corner Bookstore is open Monday to Friday from 9:00 to 5:00.

Old South Meeting House

The Old South Meeting House stands on the busy corner of Washington and Milk Streets. The original church that stood here was a small cedar building built in 1670. It was here that Judge Samuel Sewall publicly stood in shame while his "confession of contrition" was read before the congregation. The confession was for his share of guilt as a witchcraft judge in the Salem trials five years before.

(N.B.: There is a huge mural over the Speaker's desk in the State House depicting this scene.)

This was also the small chapel where Abiah Franklin brought her infant son Benjamin to be baptized only hours after he was born on a freezing cold day in January 1706. Their home was just around the corner.

The building now standing was erected in 1729 and figured prominently in the Revolutionary War period. It was the scene of town meetings too large for Faneuil Hall; and in fact, it was from here that the Boston Tea Party was launched.

The land on which the meeting house stands was given by a widow, Mary Norton, in 1669. There is a copy of her last will and testament on display here.

And thanks to another woman, Mary Hemenway, the building remains intact today. In 1876 Mary Hemenway, a leading philanthropist of the day, discovered that a group of her father's friends were conspiring to sell the Old South Meeting House. Thereupon she pledged $100,000 — half the amount needed — to save it from destruction. She followed with an organized study program to use the building as an institute to promote interest in American history.

The building continues to be used for such purposes and is a museum as well, with many relics of early Boston. Among the items on display is the rare first edition of the book of poetry by Phillis Wheatley, a young girl brought to Boston as a slave. The Wheatley family brought her to church here, and she became a member. She began writing poetry at the age of thirteen and was the second American woman to have her poetry published.

There is also a very large model showing what the city looked like at the time of the Boston Tea Party in 1775. It was done by Annie Howen Thwing in 1922.

PHILLIS WHEATLEY
Ca. 1755–1784

Should you, My Lord, while you peruse my song
Wonder from whence my love of freedom sprung,
Whence, flow these wishes for the common good,
By feeling hearts alone best understood,
I, young in life, by seeming cruel fate
Was snatch'd from Afric's seeming happy seat:
What pangs excruciating must molest —
What sorrows labor in my parent's breast?
Steel'd was that soul and by no misery mov'd
That from a father seiz'ed a babe belov'd.
Such, such my case. And can I then but pray
Others may never feel tyrannic sway.

(from an address to Lord Dartmouth, secretary to the colonies in North America)

Phillis Wheatley was born in Africa and sold as a slave in Boston in 1761. The family that bought her, the Wheatleys, soon noticed that she quickly learned to read and write. Mrs. Wheatley saw to it that Phillis was given the best education possible.

At a very young age she began writing poetry, and by the time she was nineteen, her first book of poetry was published. The book created quite a stir, and questions were raised as to whether or not she was a fraud. The Wheatley family was forced to ask for a trial to prove she was not.

Phillis was brought before a group of eighteen Boston men (John Hancock was among them) and answered a list of their questions on scripture, Latin, and classical mythology. Her quick answers and sharp intellect so astonished and convinced them that they willingly signed a document acknowledging that she had indeed written the book.

When Phillis was twenty-four years old, Mrs. Wheatley died, leaving her a free woman, but with little means to support herself. She drifted into an unfortunate marriage to a man who abused her and sold her poetry and papers to buy food and fuel. Her first two babies died; and shortly after giving birth to a third, she and the child both died.

Phillis was buried with her child in her arms in an unmarked grave in the churchyard of Old South Church.

Old State House

On the corner of State and Washington Streets, at a noisy, bustling intersection, the little Old State House, dating from 1713, stands in resolute defiance against the towering modern edifices surrounding it.

During Colonial days this was the center of town, the market and gathering place, and the spot where the first pillory and the whipping post were placed before they were moved to the Common. Just before the Revolution the square became a political arena where agitated citizens held many protests against the increasing British tyranny.

The most historic of these was, of course, the Boston Massacre, which was later to be called the first military action of the Revolution. The spot where the first patriot was felled has been commemorated with a circle of cobblestones placed right in the middle of this still perilous intersection. Caution in viewing this memorial is strongly advised, lest you yourself become part of Boston's history.

The Old State House is now a museum maintained by the Bostonian Society and contains many artifacts of the Revolutionary War period. John Hancock, the first elected governor of Massachusetts, was inaugurated here; and many of his personal belongings and those of his wife, "Dorothy Q.", are on display.

From the small balcony on the front, many important speeches were made. The proclamation repealing the Stamp Act was read from here in 1766, the Declaration of Independence in 1776, and the Proclamation of Peace in 1783. Also from here George Washington addressed a jubilant throng of Bostonians on his last visit to the city in 1789.

Almost two hundred years later, in honor of America's Bicentennial, Queen Elizabeth II, England's first reigning monarch ever to come to Boston, stood just below the same balcony and spoke to another crowd of cheering Bostonians. Reflecting on how the patriots might have reacted to her visit she said, "I think they would have been extremely surprised. But perhaps they would also have been pleased. Pleased to know that eventually we came together again as free peoples and friends and defended together the very ideals for which the American Revolution was fought."

The museum has a particularly nice gift shop specializing in Boston memorabilia, and a good collection of books on New England.

The Old State House is open every day. Summer (April through Oct.) hours are 9:30–5:00; and winter (Nov. through March) 10:00 to 4:00 on weekdays, and until 5:00 p.m. on Saturday and Sunday.

Faneuil Hall

Originally built in 1742 and remodeled several times, this is the building that John Adams dubbed "The Cradle of Liberty."

It was given to the city by merchant Peter Faneuil as a marketplace and a meeting house. The second-floor meeting hall, which in the eighteenth century was the site of many fiery pre-Revolutionary speeches, continues to be a forum for public debate today.

In the latter part of the nineteenth century the Massachusetts Woman Suffrage Association held their own fiery meetings and conventions here. At one of them, the 120th anniversary of the Boston Tea Party, William Lloyd Garrison, a noted crusader for both abolitionism and woman suffrage, recited a lengthy poem which said in part: "I'm one of those who pitched the tea as you must well remember / Into the water of the bay that seventeenth of December / But ever since I've felt remorse to think the execution / Of that cool plan to save our rights omitted thought of woman!"

The lower level of Faneuil Hall has continued throughout its existence to be a marketplace. Early ledgers belonging to Peter Faneuil show that he had many accounts with Boston tradeswomen, some of whom bought many thousand pounds' worth of imported goods in a year.

Today, businesswomen continue to operate in large numbers in a variety of small businesses throughout the Marketplace. This area has become one of the most popular places to shop, eat, and browse, as well as to be entertained at any given moment by musical and small theater groups, mime, jugglers, and dancers.

For a more extensive listing of activities here see the shopping section under Quincy Marketplace. Faneuil Hall is open daily from 9:00 a.m. to 5:00 p.m., as are most of the stores in the Marketplace. But the activity continues well into the night in the restaurants and bars.

North End

Part of the Freedom Trail winds through the North End, as there are several important historical landmarks in this small and compact district. The first landmark is in North Square: the oldest house still extant in Boston, built in the seventeenth century, where both Sara and Rachel Revere lived and gave birth to most of their sixteen children (eight apiece).

Sara and Rachel were the first and second wives of Paul Revere, who you may recall was the man best known for his famous ride "on the eighteenth of April, in seventy-five. . ." Sara died here after the birth of her eighth child in 1773, and soon after, Revere married Rachel who gave birth to eight more children.

The house is authentically furnished as it might have appeared during the historical period of the Boston Tea Party in 1773 and Paul's ride through the countryside to warn the people that the British were coming. The original beams are in place and one panel of the original wallpaper remains. The original plaster, made from clam and oyster shells, is preserved in the old kitchen.

There is also a wonderful sampler by Maria Revere Curtis, Rachel and Paul's granddaughter, which she did in 1819 when she was eleven years old.

Not far from the Revere house, on Richmond Street, is the site of the birthplace of Charlotte Cushman, the first great American actress. She excelled in interpreting male Shakespearian roles during the mid-1800s, and was as successful on the English stage as she was in America. For many years there was a girls' school on Prince Street named in her honor — the Charlotte Cushman School — but all that remains now is a gym for high-school students.

Sophie Tucker, the "Last of the Red Hot Mamas," lived at 22 Salem Street and attended the Cushman School. She made her first appearance as an actress at the "Old Howard" in Boston.

Another famous woman born in the North End was Harriot K. Hunt, one of the first women to practice medicine in this country. She began her practice in 1835, having tried and failed to get into Harvard Medical School. When she applied for a second time, in 1850, she was accepted. The male students, however, so strongly objected to her presence — saying "We object to having the company of any female forced upon us, who is disposed to unsex herself, and to sacrifice her modesty by appearing with men in the lecture room" — that she withdrew.

The incident drew national attention, and the Female Medical College of Philadelphia granted her an honorary degree of Doctor of Medicine in 1853. She continued to practice in Boston until her death in 1875.

Not far from the Revere house is the brick tenement building at 4 Garden Court in which Rose Fitzgerald Kennedy was born in 1890. Following the potato famine in Ireland in 1824, Irish immigrants had flocked to Boston via Cunard steamers and disembarked in Boston where they settled in the North End. Rose's father, "Honey Fitz," who was eventually to become mayor of Boston, was among them.

While no monument has yet been dedicated to Rose — the matriarch of a family that produced a United States president, an attorney general, a senator, and several philanthropic women — the former Kennedy home at 83 Beals Street in Brookline, where she brought up her own family, is a touching tribute to this remarkable woman. (See page 154.)

A short distance from Garden Court, crossing over Hanover Street, you'll come to the North Bennet Street Industrial School. It was founded in 1881 by Pauline Agassiz Shaw to give public-school children classes in cooking, printing, and metal- and woodworking skills.

Mrs. Shaw, who had five children of her own, was dedicated to the education of young people. Her early work in establishing nursery schools and kindergartens for children of working mothers led her to see the need for industrial skills for older children, particularly among the flood of immigrant families in the North End.

The North Bennet Street Industrial School pioneered in so many areas of manual and industrial training, as well as home arts, that it became the prototype for such schools all over the country.

The Industrial School was also the site for one of the earliest branch libraries for the North End, and Edith Guerrier, its librarian, started a group for young girls here called the Saturday Evening Girls. As part of their activities they began a workshop in pottery.

The girls became so adept at pottery that Mrs. James Storrow, wife of a prominent Boston banker, bought a house for the girls in 1912. A full-scale business began. Not only was the pottery sold nationally but Queen Mary of England ordered a set as well. Today pieces of this pottery (Paul Revere Pottery) are valuable collector's items.

The Old North Church on Salem Street (Christ Church is its real name) was built in 1723, and is the oldest house of worship still standing in Boston. It is also where the first Sunday school began in 1815.

It was here that the lanterns were hung in 1775 to signal ("one if by land, two if by sea") that the British were advancing toward Concord. The lantern-hanging and the midnight ride of Paul Revere are reenacted every year on the eve of Patriots' Day in April.

Just inside the church, on the wall to the right, is a plaque in honor of Matilda Frances Bibbey (1868–1938). She was a much beloved member of the North End community who was for many years the principal of the Charlotte Cushman School on Prince Street.

Up the hill from "Old North" is Copp's Hill Burying Ground, the second oldest cemetery in Boston, dating back to 1659. Here lies a paradox. Buried in the old Mather family tomb, in 1728, was the fiery Puritan minister, Cotton Mather. It was his writings that helped to fan the wave of hysterical fear which in turn brought about the Salem witch trials. Buried in the same crypt, one hundred years later, was his granddaughter, Hannah Mather Crocker. Hannah was the author of one of the earliest feminist tracts, *Observations on the Real Rights of Women*, written in 1818.

ANNE POLLARD
1620–1725

Anne Pollard, the first woman to land in Boston, had her picture painted when she was 100 years old. She lived to be 105.

Ten years after Mary Chilton laid claim to being the first Pilgrim to step ashore on Plymouth Rock, another young woman was to seek a similar honor as the first Puritan to land in Boston.

When John Winthrop and his stout band of Puritans sailed into Massachusetts Bay in 1630, they originally chose the land near the mouth of the Charles River for their new colony, calling it Charlestown. They soon discovered, however, that fresh water was in short supply; and they decided to move their settlement across the peninsula to the site now known as Boston.

The first longboat pulled ashore on an early summer day in June, and a "romping" ten-year-old girl named Anne Pollard was the first to skip ashore. She was later to describe her early impressions of Boston as a land "very uneven, abounding in small hollows and swamps, covered with blueberries and other bushes."

In spite of the fact that the first harsh winter took its toll on the settlers, claiming the lives of over two hundred (about one in five), Anne

134

Pollard survived them all by living to be 105. She had a large (and prolific) family, the youngest of her thirteen children being born when Anne was 58 years old.

Anne and her husband kept an inn at the corner of Beacon and Charles Streets called the Horse Shoe Tavern. Long after her husband's death, surviving him by almost fifty years, Anne continued to run the business. The tavern was a favorite haunt of Harvard students; and here on the wide front porch on summer nights, Anne, smoking her clay pipe, would regale the boys with stories of old England.

When she died in 1725, over one hundred and thirty-five of her descedants attended her funeral, as well as a large contingent of Harvard students. Her great-grandchild Robbie, who had died a few days previously, was laid in her arms for burial.

Her portrait, which was painted when she was 100 years old, hangs in the Massachusetts Historical Society (1154 Boylston Street), and is the only one in existence of a woman of the first generation of Bostonians.

Although the Horse Shoe Inn is no longer standing at the corner of Beacon and Charles streets, a monument commemorating Anne's famous arrival is not far from the scene. At the entrance to the Common on Beacon Street across from Spruce Street, there is a bas-relief depicting Anne along with John Winthrop and others landing on the shores of Boston.

TOURS OF VICTORIAN BEACON HILL AND BACK BAY

Walking tours of Boston abound. There are harbor walks, art walks, "heart of the hub" walks, architectural walks, Victorian walks, *Make Way for Ducklings* walks, Kennedy-roots walks — just name your interest and one of the Visitor Information Centers will direct you to the right tour guide.

Other than the Freedom Trail walk, however, the two most popular areas for an interesting stroll are Beacon Hill and the Back Bay. They're the most historic and the most picturesque, and probably were the backdrop for your favorite book, play, movie, or TV sitcom set in Boston.

In either of these neighborhoods you hardly need a guide to roam around with you to point out the beautiful black lace of wrought-iron balconies, the unusual purple-paned windows, or the handsome Colonial doorways with their large, shiny brass knockers.

But, as this is also the area where some of the most important liter-

ary figures of the past two centuries lived, you might like to know who
lived where — particularly since many of them were women.

Beacon Hill

A good place to start a walking tour of Beacon Hill is at the Nichols
House Museum at the top of Mount Vernon Street at number 55. This
was the former home of Rose Standish Nichols — landscape architect,
author of books on gardening, world traveler, founder of intellectual
clubs for women, and the epitome of what authors such as John Mar-
quand and Cleveland Amory like to call Boston's grande dame.

Born in 1872, she was the eldest of three daughters of Dr. and Mrs.
Arthur H. Nichols. She never married and upon her death willed the
house to be used as a museum. It is the prototype of the Beacon Hill
home of the early part of this century.

For years her home was a salon where important international visitors to Boston came and mingled with noted local scholars. Rose Nichols was an early supporter of the Women's International League for
Peace and Freedom and the League of Small Nations. It is not surprising, therefore, that the first floor of the museum is now occupied by the
Boston Center for International Visitors, which plays host each year to
many visitors from all over the world.

The museum is furnished with the personal belongings of Mrs.
Nichols and her family and has been kept just the way it was when she
lived there. There are some period pieces belonging to the Nichols
family as well as other treasures that Rose gathered on her world travels.

It is also filled with fine examples of her needlework, such as crewel
bed hangings and drapes, needlepoint pictures and pillows, and a
lovely petitpoint fireplace screen. Mrs. Nichols also studied woodworking and made several excellent copies of Jacobean furniture which
are on display.

The museum is open Monday, Wednesday, and Saturday from 1:00
to 5:00 p.m. (closed Sundays and holidays).

Author Lilian Aldrich was a friend and neighbor of Mrs. Nichols
and lived a few houses away at number 59 Mount Vernon. It was at the
Beacon Hill Reading Club, which Mrs. Nichols founded (and presided
over for almost sixty years), that Lilian read chapters of her books to
the supportive and encouraging members.

Julia Ward Howe, founder and president of many local and national
women's clubs, social reformer, and author (most widely renowned for

her writing of the Civil War song "Battle Hymn of the Republic") lived at two different houses on Mount Vernon Street — numbers 32 and 48.

The stately house at number 85 was one of the three houses built in 1801 for a prominent Boston family, the Harrison Gray Otises. The house has acquired more fame, however, in recent years by being the site of such movies as *The Thomas Crown Affair* and the television show "Banacek."

Noted sculptor Anne Whitney lived and worked at 92 Mount Vernon. It was here that she executed her statue of Leif Ericson, erected on Commonwealth Avenue in 1887. In 1875 she had won first place in an anonymous competition for a memorial to Charles Sumner (abolitionist and United States senator). She was denied the commission when the judges discovered that she was a woman.

She continued working well into her late seventies, sculpting many famous women and men of the day. Her final piece was completed when she was eighty. It was made from the early model of Charles Sumner whose coveted prize she had never been given. The statue now stands in a prominent spot in Cambridge overlooking Harvard Square.

Diarist Alice James lived for a short time at number 131, where she aided her brother Henry in nursing their older brother William back to health after he had been wounded in the Civil War.

Halfway down Mount Vernon Street is one of the prettiest spots on the hill, and probably the most photographed, Louisburg Square (always pronounced "Lew-is").

There are twenty-two houses surrounding a small fenced-in common here, and all the "proprietors" are bound by an ancient agreement to keep up the premises. Every time the trees in the common are trimmed, so they say, the wood is divided into twenty-two little bundles and delivered to each house for fireplace burning.

Many famous people have lived in the square since it was completed in 1834. Among them was Louisa May Alcott, who owned number 10. It was here that her father, Bronson Alcott, died; and Louisa, ill in a nearby nursing home, died a few days later.

Jenny Lind married her accompanist Otto Goldschmidt at number 20, and they lived here happily for many years.

Passing through Louisburg Square you enter Pinckney Street, home to numerous Boston literati over the years. The Alcotts had previously lived at number 20, where Louisa did some of her early writing.

Little Ms. Beacon Street
sat on her window seat,
eating her beans and brown
bread;
There came a small spider
and sat down beside her
"You're an Argyroneta,"
she said.

Anonymous

Elizabeth Peabody started the first formally organized kindergarten in the country on Pinckney Street. Parents such as Julia Ward Howe paid one dollar a week to send their children to the school, which was located first at number 13 and later at number 15.

Abbie Brown, poet and author of children's books, also lived on Pinckney Street. She was the coauthor of "On the Trail," the official song of the Girl Scouts.

Alice Brown, a prolific writer of novels set in New England, lived at number 11. She was also the cofounder of the Women's Rest Tour Association (now Travelers Information Exchange), an organization dedicated to assisting women travelers.

Nathaniel Hawthorne lived at number 54 during one of his unsuccessful periods of writing. Surrounded as he was on Pinckney Street by so many talented women, it is easy to see why he complained to his publisher, "America is now wholly given over to a damned mob of scribbling women."

Number 62 Pinckney was the home of Mr. and Mrs. George Hillard during the days of the Underground Railroad. Mrs. Hillard was an ardent abolitionist, and, unbeknown to her husband, she hid fugitive slaves behind a secret trap door in an upstairs ceiling. Her husband was a United States commissioner whose job was to issue warrants for the arrest of fugitive slaves!

On the corner of Mount Vernon and Charles Streets is the newly renovated but very old Charles Street Meeting House. It was originally a Baptist church. When it was first built in 1807, the river came almost up to the church making baptisms in the Charles River very convenient.

The Meeting House became a forum in the 1850s for many antislavery speakers such as Harriet Tubman and Sojourner Truth; and as late as the 1960s it continued to serve as an assembly hall for social-protest meetings. It is now privately owned and is used as a residence and office space with several shops on the street level.

Lucretia Hale, author of *The Peterkin Papers*, lived down Charles Street at number 127 with her brother Edward Everett Hale.

Toward the end of Charles Street, on the site where a parking garage now stands, was number 148 Charles, the home of author Annie Adams Fields. Here she and her husband Jamie Fields, publisher, editor, and proprietor of the Old Corner Bookstore, held what was considered one of the most important literary salons in Boston in the nineteenth century in their home. They entertained such eminent authors as Harriet Beecher Stowe, Celia Thaxter, Henry Wadsworth Longfellow, Charles Dickens, and many others.

Many of these same authors joined Margaret Fuller, Lydia Marie Child, Lucretia Mott, and others at the famous Radical Club which was called "one of the intellectual landmarks of Boston" between 1867 and 1880. They were Monday-morning meetings held at the home of the Reverend and Mrs. John Sargent on Chestnut Street for intellectual discussions.

Chestnut Street, at the other end of Charles Street, has some of the loveliest single-family homes left on the hill, with deeply recessed and ornate doorways. The houses at numbers 13, 15, and 17 are called the "daughters" houses because they were built by Hepzibah Swan for her three daughters. Mrs. Swan was the only woman among the Mt. Vernon proprietors, the early developers of Beacon Hill.

Another famous Boston grande dame lived on Chestnut Street, Helen Choate Bell, often called "the complete Boston woman." She was known for her wit and her often irreverent comments on Boston society. No book on Boston would be complete without one of her oft-quoted one-liners. It was she who said of the newly invented

Louisa May Alcott lived at Number 10 Louisburg Square.

automobile that "it would soon divide mankind into two classes, the quick and the dead."

The north slope of Beacon Hill (turning left at the top of Pinckney) was the heart of the black community for a number of years. The Black Heritage Trail begins just off Joy Street on Smith Court.

The Old African Meeting House is located here; it was the first black church in Boston and an early educational center. The Abiel Smith School, next door, was the first public school for black children in Boston.

A detailed brochure of the Black Heritage Trail is available at the Visitor Information Centers.

Walking down the other side of the hill on Joy Street and turning right onto Beacon Street, you will come to the twin buildings of numbers 39 and 40. In the second-floor drawing room at Number 39, Fanny Appleton married poet Henry Wadsworth Longfellow in 1843. It is still a romantic spot for weddings and is often used as such.

The Women's City Club of Boston has been located here almost since its founding in 1913. As in several other houses along Beacon Street and throughout the hill, you will notice several purple window-panes in the front windows. Some glass that was imported from England around 1820 contained too much manganese, which created this color. The purple panes are one of the original status symbols of the hill, and much prized by their owners.

Another set of twin bowfront houses almost next door to the Women's City Club, at numbers 50 and 55, were built for Boston merchant James Smith Colburn and his sister in 1808.

Number 55 is now headquarters for the National Society of The Colonial Dames of America in the Commonwealth of Massachusetts, and is called the William Hickling Prescott House in honor of the nineteenth-century historian who lived and wrote there.

The house, which is opened to the public on Wednesdays from 10:00 to 4:00, is filled with some of the original Colburn furniture as well as many added antique pieces. There is also a fine collection of China-trade porcelain, English ceramics, and some very nice examples of early needlework.

A documented costume collection dating from the eighteenth century to the present is housed here, and periodically selections from it are on display. Prescott's library has been preserved much as he left it, with all of his first editions neatly arranged.

Tours are given on Wednesday by one of the Colonial Dames, or you can arrange for an appointment by calling 742-3190.

The hill is particularly festive during the Christmas holidays, when the homes are ablaze with candles in the windows, carolers sing, and the Beacon Hill Hand Bell Ringers give a Christmas Eve concert in Louisburg Square.

As you cross Beacon Street at the corner of Charles, heading toward the Public Garden, you'll be following the famous path of yet another well-known "lady," Mrs. Mallard.

It was here that the heroine of *Make Way for Ducklings* brought the busy Beacon Street traffic to a halt while she led her family to the safety of the pond in the Public Garden.

Back Bay

Ironically, the Back Bay, the epitome of Boston's wealthy Victorian society in the 1800s, was built on an odorous and insect-infested swamp. Tons of fill had to be carted all the way into Boston from Needham to cure the city's worst health hazard. What surprisingly resulted was over five hundred acres of prime real estate, where some of the most palatial mansions in Boston were built.

The Back Bay is the easiest part of the city to find your way around in because the cross streets starting at the Public Garden are alphabetically named. Not only are they alphabetical, but for a bit of whimsy, you may notice that they alternate disyllables with trisyllables: Arl-ing-ton, Berke-ley, Clar-en-don, Dart-mouth, and so on.

Needless to say, this area was carefully and thoughtfully laid out. Commonwealth Avenue, with its grassy central mall copied from the French, is the Back Bay's main boulevard; and many of the houses still have the French-inspired facades that were popular at the time.

Now, however, most of these once proud homes have been turned into apartments and condominiums. In fact, less than 15 percent of the buildings in the Back Bay area remain as one-family homes today.

Beacon Street extends from the hill into Back Bay and has long been considered one of the elite Boston addresses — providing you're on the "right" side of the street. The river side is, of course, the preferred location. Before Storrow Drive was built in the 1930s, the back lawns from these houses extended to the embankment.

As on Commonwealth Avenue, many of the Beacon Street houses have now been broken up into apartments or converted to institutional uses.

The Gibson House at 137 Beacon Street is a good place to start a walking tour of the Back Bay. Not only was this one of the first houses to be built in the Back Bay, but it has been preserved just the way it was at the turn of the century and is now one of the few houses in the neighborhood open to the public.

The house was built by Katherine Hammond Gibson in 1859. Her husband, a sea merchant, had died at sea, leaving her and her young son amply provided for. The house is typically Victorian and elegantly decorated with silks, tapestry, frescoes, and rich wallpapers. The furniture is elaborately ornamented as was the custom then and is mixed with some early-American and English family heirlooms.

Dark woodwork, marble fireplaces, and multiflowered patterns are prevalent throughout this six-floor townhouse. The house is open from May through October on Tuesday through Sunday from 2:00 to 5:00 p.m., and from November through April on Saturday and Sunday from 2:00 to 5:00 p.m. Tours are scheduled at 2:00, 3:00, and 4:00, and you are admitted to the house only at these times; so don't get there too early.

Across from the Gibson House at number 118 Beacon is the main building of Fisher Junior College. This was formerly the sumptuous home of Mr. and Mrs. Henry P. King. Many of the features of the house are Roman: marble floors and fireplaces, wall niches for statuary, paired columns, gold cornices. But the most outstanding attraction is the marble hanging stairway with a twenty-four-karat gold-plated balustrade that graces the reception hall.

Carved rosewood doors with sterling silver knobs, walnut-paneled walls, Wedgwood-style ceilings, silver and crystal chandeliers, and the original hand-woven Burmese rugs give evidence of the wealth of Victorian Back Bay.

Fisher Junior College is primarily a secretarial school for young women, and they have nicely blended their modern equipment with the plush surroundings. Students give tours upon request, but phone ahead for an appointment (262-3240).

Before Isabella Stewart Gardner built her palace in the Fens, she lived at number 152 Beacon Street where, it has been said, she entertained lavishly.

In 1880 she bought number 150 in order to add a music room and a ballroom to her home. When she moved to Fenway Court in 1903, she sold the house with the stipulation that the number 152 never be used again. It is now 150 Beacon Street.

In 1879, after her husband died, Julia Ward Howe moved from her Beacon Hill home to an apartment in the house at 241 Beacon Street. Here she continued to write and lecture and became a close friend of her neighbor, Mrs. Gardner.

A third parallel street running through the heart of the Back Bay is Newbury, where the houses have all been converted into fashionable boutiques, cafes, and art galleries. Above one of the shops at 35 Newbury, you can still see three floors with unusually large bay windows.

This was the home of author Margaret Deland. Every year she planted boxes of daffodils and jonquils in these windows and, in the late winter, held a flower sale. The proceeds were given to her favorite project, a vacation home for girls.

At number 15 Newbury Street you'll find the beautiful Leslie Lindsey Memorial Chapel which adjoins the Emmanuel Church. Leslie Lindsey, the daughter of a wealthy Boston businessman, was on her honeymoon aboard the ill-fated *Lusitania* on May 7, 1915. When it sank off the Irish coast after being torpedoed by a German submarine, her body — along with those of almost two thousand other passengers — was recovered. She was still wearing the ruby and diamond jewels that her father had given her as a wedding present. Her parents sold the jewels to build this lovely Gothic chapel, which was completed in 1924. The best time to visit is on a Sunday morning when the church is open to visitors.

The Exeter Street Theatre at the corner of Newbury Street was originally built as a temple for the Progressive Spiritualists, but was converted to a theater in 1935. It is the oldest continuously running movie theater in Boston. For many years it was run by two well-educated sisters, Viola and Florence Berlin. The Berlins chose only the best movies — thought-provoking or family-oriented rather than Westerns or

Author Margaret Deland planted daffodils and jonquils in her large windows at number 35 Newbury Street. She held an annual winter flower sale to raise money for a girls' summer vacation camp.

slapstick comedies. As a result it became a favorite theater with Boston women, who attended so regularly that the proprietors were on a first-name basis with most of their customers. Although now under new ownership, it continues to show exceptionally good movies and ones that aren't shown elsewhere in Boston.

A few blocks up Newbury and around the corner on Hereford Street at number 40, the famous cooking school of Fannie Farmer was housed. Her cookbook, *Boston Cooking School Cook Book*, contained the first recipes using standard level measurements.

The book was originally turned down by the publisher, Little, Brown, and Co., until Miss Farmer offered to pay the publishing costs. It has since sold over four million copies and has been translated into several languages, making the name of Fannie Farmer a household word.

There are several events throughout the year that have become part of Back Bay tradition. The lighting of the trees on Boston Common the week before Christmas; the Back Bay street fair on Marlborough Street in early June; the Easter Parade on Commonwealth Avenue on Easter Sunday; Art Newbury Street in the spring and the fall; and the most celebrated event in Boston — which brings almost all Back Bay activity to a halt on the third Monday in April — the running of the Boston Marathon, with the finish line at the Prudential Center.

ELIZABETH GLENDOWER EVANS
1856–1937

Elizabeth Glendower Evans defied her Boston Brahmin relatives and joined in helping the Lawrence textile strikers win their victory.

Elizabeth Glendower Evans was a pioneer in social reform and helped make Massachusetts a leader in progressive penal techniques. In 1912 she led the Massachusetts campaign which resulted in the first minimum-wage act for women in the United States. During the 1920s she became a national director of the American Civil Liberties Union defending free speech and the rights of aliens.

Although born to a proper Bostonian family, Elizabeth was to become a "poor relation" upon the accidental death of her father. Her dependency upon relatives at an early age instilled in her a strong compassion for the underdog, and she was to champion many such causes throughout her life.

She shocked her relatives by taking part in the labor strikes in Roxbury in 1910 and later at the textile mills in Lawrence. Here she joined picket lines, provided bail funds, and was eventually jailed herself for leading picket marches in front of the mills. The *Boston Transcript* blatantly called her "a degenerate decadent of the Back Bay."

But of all her accomplishments

and causes, nothing was to propel her into the limelight as much as her close association with the Sacco-Van-zetti case, Boston's infamous trial of two Italian immigrants accused and convicted of murder.

It was largely through her involve-ment that the trial gained such na-tional attention. She enlisted the aid of prominent trial lawyers, contrib-uted time and money to the defense, and published articles about the case in national magazines.

Firmly believing that these two men had been convicted on a wave of anti-alien hysteria, she fought for over six years to stay their execution. Although her efforts were in vain (Sacco's last words at the execution, "Farewell Mother," were for her), she roused national sympathy and un-derstanding for the rights of aliens.

The debates over the Sacco-Van-zetti case continue to this day; and in Upton Sinclair's popular novel, *Bos-ton*, the heroine is largely modeled on the part that Elizabeth Evans played in this historic trial.

CAMBRIDGE, THE CITY ACROSS THE CHARLES

Cambridge is unmistakably a city disparate from Boston. It offers a wide variety of accommodations, restaurants, entertainment and his-torical landmarks of its own. Because this book is geared toward the visitor and relocator with a minimum of time, we have included here only a brief overview of this rich and colorful city just across the Charles River from Boston.

Cambridge is so inextricably linked to Boston that it's often thought of as one of the neighborhoods. In fact, you can get from downtown Boston to Cambridge on the MBTA faster (eight or nine minutes) than to such far-flung Boston neighborhoods as Jamaica Plain or Matta-pan.

But Cambridge is definitely a city in its own right and with a distinct flavor of its own to boot. Dominated by three of the most prestigious educational institutions in the country, Radcliffe, Harvard, and Mas-sachusetts Institute of Technology, plus numerous other colleges and private schools, Cambridge has naturally maintained over the years a large student population. And the constant influx of young people to the Harvard Square area has created a district that merely grows older each year — but never quite grows up. The boutiques and shops clut-tering the Square are devoted to youthful needs and wants — school supplies, vintage "dress-up" or "prep" clothes, nostalgic toys and games, ice cream and cookies, and block furniture painted in bright colors.

Coffee houses such as Passim (Joan Baez got her start here) still abound, along with innumerable cafes, bars, and fast-food take-out places. Also, the city's high concentration of ethnic groups in the working-class neighborhoods of North Cambridge, East Cambridge, and Cambridgeport generates an abundance of ethnic and vegetarian restaurants in the Central Square area as well as Harvard Square.

Cambridge was founded in 1630 and was the site from which Washington commanded his troops in 1775; and it follows that this city is just as steeped in American history as Boston. It also follows that many illustrious women were a significant part of that history.

Cambridge was home to Elizabeth Glover, who established the first printing press in America (although her husband who died en route to America was later given the credit). Martha Washington, who called the General "old man," slept here at 105 Brattle Street. Margaret Fuller, who wrote the first major feminist tract in America and who also became the country's first woman foreign correspondent, was born here.

Elizabeth Agassiz not only established Radcliffe College here in 1879, she also became its first president. She had to drape her classroom windows so that Harvard professors would not be seen teaching women!

Margaret Taussig, also born in Cambridge, was not permitted to take obstetrics and gynecology in the mid-1920s at Harvard Medical School ("they were subjects that women should know nothing about!" she said) so she took bacteriology and histology instead and went on to pioneer in open-heart surgery.

There were hundreds of other equally brilliant women from this city, and even today hardly a week goes by during the academic year when one of the current leaders isn't holding forth from her podium somewhere in Cambridge.

There's plenty to do here too, whether it's touring one of the campuses, dropping into one of the cafes, or just browsing in the shops. (For antiques and "fleas" there are any number of such shops all along Massachusetts Avenue, north of Harvard Square.) Some interesting tours:

Radcliffe and Harvard College Information Office in the lobby of Holyoke Center, Harvard Square (campus map available); or in Admission Office, Byerly Hall, 8 Garden Street.

MARGARET FULLER
1810–1850

Margaret Fuller: "It is a vulgar error that love, a love, to women is her whole existence; she is also born for Truth and Love in their universal energy." (The Dial, *1843*)

Margaret Fuller, author of the first major feminist publication in America, *Woman in the Nineteenth Century*, was born in Cambridge in 1810.

She was the oldest of nine children; and her father, disappointed that his firstborn was not a boy, was determined, nevertheless, that she should be treated as an equal. Her formal education began almost at birth and she was reciting Latin verse by the age of seven. By the time she was a teenager she had read her way through her father's extensive library and could talk on any subject.

It is not surprising that even among such literary giants of the day as Emerson, Thoreau, Hawthorne, and Greeley, she was to become an important leader. She was fully accepted into the Boston intellectual community and after several years of teaching became the editor of *The Dial* in 1840. It was one of the most highly respected publications of its day, and most of the significant writers of that period contributed to it.

At the home of her friend Elizabeth Peabody, on West Street, she held her famous Conversations.

These were Wednesday-afternoon discussion groups devoted to such topics as art, ethics, education, and women's rights, and attracted the most influential women in Boston.

In 1884 Margaret Fuller was invited by Horace Greeley to come to New York to become a writer and critic for the *Daily Tribune.* She later became a foreign correspondent (the first woman in America to do so) and traveled through Europe sending reports back to the *Tribune.*

While in Italy she fell in love with and married an Italian nobleman and became deeply committed to the cause of Italian independence. She wrote a book on the Roman Revolution and, when unable to get clear copyrights in Europe, decided to return to America.

She and her husband and their small son sailed for home, but their ship was wrecked in a storm just outside New York harbor and all three were drowned. Only the body of her son was recovered, and he was buried in Mount Auburn Cemetery in Cambridge.

Margaret Fuller's birthplace, her home at 17 Cherry Street in Cambridge, has been a settlement house since 1902. Responding to the needs of women and children in the community through child care, tutoring, and educational and social opportunities, it is affectionately referred to as "Marga."

Massachusetts Institute of Technology   77 Massachusetts Avenue, Admissions Office, Building 3, Room 108 (253-1000).

Feminist Tour of Cambridge   Harvard University, Women's Center, Lehman Hall, Harvard Yard. Meeting place, resource center, library, information on groups and activities for women as well as a list of Harvard administrators and faculty involved with women's issues.

Historic Walk of Cambridge   (Get free map at Information Office, Holyoke Center lobby.) From Harvard Square walk along Brattle Street, named for loyalist William Brattle (who fled Boston in 1774), to number 42. Margaret Fuller lived here during the time she was editing the *Dial,* and it now houses the Cambridge Center for Adult Education. Brattle Street, nicknamed "Tory Row" in pre-Revolutionary days, is lined with many beautiful old houses, some dating back to the early 1800s. Number 105 was the home of poet Henry Wadsworth Longfellow, his wife Fanny, and their three daughters, "grave Alice," "laughing Allegra," and "Edith with golden hair." You can tour the first floor of the house (it's open every day from 10:00 a.m. to 4:30 p.m.), where daughter Alice preserved her father's study just the way it was when she descended the stairs. The houses at 113 and 115 belonged to Edith and Allegra and their families. A little farther up Brattle at number 159 is the oldest house still standing in Cambridge, the Lee-Nichols House, where the Cambridge Historical Society is located. The house is open to the public every Thursday from 3:00 to 5:00, and during the summer on Monday from 3:00 to 5:00 as well. Back toward Harvard Square on Brattle Street, you'll come to the Blacksmith House at number 56. This was the site of Longfellow's "spreading chestnut tree" where the "village smithy" stood. It is now a tearoom and pastry shop (alfresco in the warm weather) and a perfect place for a light lunch or snack. Another delightful spot for a quiet lunch in this area is at Passim, 47 Palmer Court (behind the Harvard Coop), where you can have a delicious bowl of homemade soup or a sandwich, listen to recorded classical music, and read the paper at leisure.

Mount Auburn Cemetery   This may sound dreary, but it's not. It is filled with beautiful trees and gardens; in fact, they have a map explaining the plantings. There is also a map available which will direct you to the tombs of such illustrious dead as Mary Baker Eddy, Fannie Farmer, Amy Lowell, Harriot K. Hunt, Julia Ward Howe, Margaret Fuller, Dorothea Dix, Josephine Ruffin, Isabella Stewart Gardner, and a host of others.

WHAT TO DO ON SUNDAY

Since most of Massachusett's "blue laws" (Puritanical rules against drinking, shopping, or working on Sundays) have now been overruled, Boston is almost as lively on Sunday afternoons as it is during the rest of the week.

Shops are open in Downtown Crossing and Faneuil Hall Marketplace and even a few in staid old Back Bay. Most sports and cultural activities also continue on Sunday. Here are a few extra Boston treats you won't want to miss:

Swan Boat   rides have been a Boston tradition since 1877. Hop aboard and be foot-pedaled around the Duck Pond in the Public Garden any time from 10:00 a.m. to 4:00 p.m. (but only from mid-April to late September).

New England Aquarium (742-8870) features the world's largest cylin-drical glass tank, which houses sharks and giant turtles, as well as countless kinds of fish. You can watch divers descend into the tank to feed these sea creatures. There are also dolphin and sea-lion shows, and there's a nice view of the harbor from the third-level lounge; and it's open from 9:00 a.m. until 6:00 p.m. on Sunday.

Bunker Hill Monument and Pavilion (241-7575) recreates the glory of the past. The monument is a 294-step walk-up that offers a great view; and nearby is the famous U.S.S. *Constitution* ("Old Ironsides"), which you can board. Museum, exhibits, slide show, and a gift shop can take a whole Sunday afternoon — til 4:00 p.m. or until 6:00 p.m. in the summer.

SARAH JOSEPHA HALE
1788–1879

Mary had a little lamb,
Its fleece was white as snow;
And everywhere that Mary went
The lamb was sure to go.

When Sarah Josepha Hale's husband died a few days before the birth of their fifth child, she immediately turned to her talent for writing to support herself and her family. Her first novel, *Northwood*, was written, she noted in the preface, "literally with my baby in my arms."

A few years later, a book of poems for children (including "Mary's Lamb") attracted the attention of a Boston publisher who invited her to become the editor of a new publication, *Ladies' Magazine*.

Ladies' Magazine, under her guidance, became so successful that a rival publisher in Philadelphia, Louis Antoine Godey, offered to purchase it. Godey wanted to combine it with his own publication and offered Mrs. Hale the job of editing the combined magazines.

Within a few years, *Godey's Lady's Book*, as it was called, broke all records for circulation, and many important writers of the day eagerly competed for space on its poetry and fiction pages. As its editor, Hale continued for over forty years to be one of the strongest influences on the life of American women.

Although she was born in New Hampshire (and was later to move to Philadelphia to edit *Godey's Lady's Book*), her Boston years were eventful and historic. She worked for the establishment of state normal schools for women, launched a fund-raising campaign to complete the Bunker Hill Monument, founded the Sea-man's Aid Society of Boston, and was active in the Boston Ladies' Peace Society.

Devoted to patriotic causes, she was instrumental in having Mount Vernon established as a national shrine. Among her many accomplishments, she is also remembered as the one who persuaded President Lincoln to declare the last Thursday in November Thanksgiving Day.

***

John Hancock Tower   (247-1977) has an observatory on the sixtieth floor with unquestionably the best view of Boston and surrounding towns as well as some breathtaking photos and films of the city. It opens at noon on Sunday for daytime views, sunsets, and starlit nights. (It closes at 11:00 p.m.)

Prudential Center   (236-3318) has generated a lot of activity on Sundays with the Hynes Auditorium and the Cheri Theatre complex close by. Also, many small shops and restaurants around here stay open all afternoon. But, of course, the biggest attraction is the "Skywalk" atop the Pru, where you'll get a 360-degree view of the city and beyond, Sundays from 10:00 a.m. until 11:00 p.m.

John F. Kennedy Birthplace National Historic Site   83 Beals St., Brookline (566-7937): While there are several memorials to the late President Kennedy in the Boston area (including his Museum and Library at Columbia Point in Dorchester, 929-4523, loaded with mementos from his White House years but noticeably lacking in mementos of his wife, Jacqueline), our favorite is the site of his birth, which is actually a tribute to his mother, Rose. Mrs. Kennedy narrates a taped tour through this surprisingly modest home, which has been restored to its 1914–1921 Kennedy days. She talks about her children and her life there while you view her small writing nook, her favorite chair, and the bed in which she gave birth to one of her sons. Open 10:00 a.m.–4:30 p.m. 7 days a week. 50 cents for adults.

Gloucester/Rockport Evening Dinner Tour   (426-8805, Gray Line bus tour) This 5½-hour late-afternoon, early-evening tour travels along the Massachusetts coastline to Cape Ann, where at the very tip of Rockport you'll visit Bearskin Neck, long a favorite artists' colony. It then takes you to Gloucester, a major fishing port, where you'll sample a traditional New England seafood dinner at the Gloucester House on the wharf. (June to September; pickup at all major Boston hotels Sundays at 4:00 p.m.)

Lexington and Concord   (426-8805, Gray Line bus tour) This three-hour tour takes you through historic Cambridge, along the route of Paul Revere's famous midnight ride to Lexington, and on to Concord. In Concord you'll see (but not stop at) the homes of Hawthorne and Emerson and "Orchard House" where Louisa May Alcott wrote *Little Women*. The tour departs from all major hotels in Boston at 2:00 p.m. on Sunday.

Plymouth Pilgrimage   (Travel Resources, 367-1980) See where Mary Chilton hopped upon the famous rock and where Priscilla Alden told John to speak for himself; and board the replica of the May-flower, where the first American citizen, Peregrine White, was born.

Salem   The Witch City (426-8805, Gray Line bus tour) Be glad you didn't live around here in 1692, when twenty women plus two dogs were executed for being "possessed by the devil." You can visit the Witch Museum and hear the gory details. Also visit Hawthorne's "House of Seven Gables" and Pickering Wharf. Drop by Crow Haven Corner where a modern-day witch, Laurie Cabot, will sell you her "Magical Power for Women" potion. This four-hour tour departs from major hotels in Boston at 12:45 p.m. on Sundays, April to October only.

Special Tours: If you're traveling to Boston with a group and need assistance in planning your activities while here, there are several good guide services available. Two that are run by experienced Boston women are The Boston Guide Service (367-1980) and Boston Proper (749-1658).

If you're traveling alone and would like to join a group for some special sightseeing, here are some suggestions.

Boston by Foot   (367-2345) gives special guided walks around town that highlight the city's history and architecture. On Sunday afternoons they have a special "tour of the month" which usually focuses on something out of the ordinary.

Boston Harbor Cruises   (227-4320) takes you on a boat tour of Boston's historic waterfront, the outer harbor, or the scenic harbor islands. These narrated cruises are either forty or ninety minutes long but, of course, are from May to September only.

Sightseeing on the Double   (739-0100) is a lectured shuttle tour on a double-decker bus of the Freedom Trail and shopping centers. The nice part of this tour is that you can get off anywhere along the way and then catch a later bus to continue on. The tour begins at the Visitor Information Center on Boston Common and your one-fare ticket ($6.00) is good all day.

"Lolly the Trolley"   consists of a one-hour narrated day tour through six miles of the city. Tickets are $4.00 (children $2.00), and the tour departs from Quincy Market 11:00 a.m. to 6:00 p.m. on Sundays.

SPORTS & FITNESS

Whether you're a spectator or an active participant, you'll find that you can take part in just about any sport in Boston. Besides the traditional ball games, bicycling, skating, or jogging, there's whale watching, curling, kite flying, dog racing, demolition derby, clamming — almost nothing is out of the question.

Sports are often front-page news here too. Some of the most exciting and important sporting events for women are held in and around the city, including the Bonne Bell 10K National Championship; an Avon Tennis Tournament; and the largest women's annual track meet in New England, the Annual Kendall Women's Classic.

And, of course, there's the Boston Marathon, which since 1972 has graciously condescended to allow women to enter this world-famous classic event.

Although Roberta Gibb ran the Boston Marathon in 1966, undetected, the whole world was to hear about Katherine Switzer, who ran it in 1967. Women were not allowed to run in the Marathon; but when K. V. Switzer filled out her application blank, the committee, not knowing she was a woman, issued her a number.

During the race, when it was discovered she was a woman, codirector Jock Semple jumped into the race and tried to pull Switzer out. She not only managed to fight Semple off, but outran him as well, to complete the race successfully.

Kay Switzer being hassled in her first Boston Marathon.

In so doing, she broke the sex barrier for women marathon runners all over the world. Since 1972 women have been entering the Boston Marathon in record numbers, and within the last few years they have been crossing the finish line a mere twenty minutes behind the winners. We're catching up fast.

Bike Rentals

Community Bike Shop, 175 Massachusetts Ave., Boston, 267-3763.

The Herson Cycle Co., 1250 Cambridge St., Cambridge, 876-4000.

Bike Touring

Appalachian Mountain Club, 5 Joy St., Boston, 523-0636. Day, weekend, and longer trips, including most winter and summer sports. Call for trip lists and schedules.

New England Bicycle Touring, P.O. Box 390, Salisbury, 1-462-3020. Weekend and two five-day tours of Cape Ann, Martha's Vineyard and other quaint and historic areas in Massachusetts.

Boating/Canoeing Rentals

Charles River Canoe Service, Commonwealth Ave., Newton, 965-5110.

The Outback Shop, 10 Mt. Auburn St., Cambridge, 491-4173 (canoe & kayak).

Jamaica Pond Boathouse, 507 Jamaicaway, Jamaica Plain, 522-4944. Rowboat rentals on Jamaica Pond, Sat. & Sun. only.

Sailing Instruction

Boston Sailing Center, 54 Lewis Wharf, Boston, 227-4198.

Boston Harbor Sailing Club, 72 E. India Row, Boston, 523-2619. One-week or weekend beginner's courses.

Fishing

For information on fishing regulations and Mass. licenses call 727-3151.

M & M Marine Service, Inc., 619 E. Broadway, S. Boston, 268-2244. Flounder and cod fishing around Boston Harbor.

Quincy Bay Flounder Fleet, 57 Taylor St., Dorchester, 773-9020. Flounder fishing around Boston Harbor.

Golf (Public Courses)

Fresh Pond Golf Club, 691 Huron Ave., Cambridge, 354-9130 (nine holes).

Norwood Country Club, 400 Province Hwy., Norwood, 769-5880 (eighteen holes). Fifteen miles from Boston.

President Golf Club, 357 W. Squantum St., Quincy, 328-3444 (eighteen holes). Eight miles from Boston.

Health, Fitness, and Exercise

Boston Park Plaza Hotel Health Club, 64 Arlington St., Boston, 542-6861. Daily exercise classes, fitness evaluation, sauna, steam, massage, and showers. Open Mon.–Thurs. 11:00 a.m. to 8:00 p.m., Fri. 11:00 a.m. to 7:00 p.m., Sat. 10:00 a.m. to 1:00 p.m., closed Sun.

Boston Center for Adult Education, 122 Arlington St., Boston, 542-1029. Total fitness workout, aerobics and exercise to music, gym, showers. Mon., Wed., Fri., noon to 1:00 p.m. One minute from T stop.

The YWCA, 7 Temple St., Cambridge, 491-6050. Keep-fit classes, drop-in volleyball and swimming. Mon.–Fri., 9:00–5:00. (Women's swim 8:00 a.m.)

New England Women's Gym, 1261 Cambridge St., Cambridge, 497-9776. Classes in aerobic fitness, self-defense, hatha yoga, body building, power lifting, and weight training; massage, nutritional guidance, shower facilities. Open Mon.–Fri. 9:00 a.m. to 9:00 p.m.; Sat. 10:00 to 3:00; Sun. 10:00 to 2:00.

Bodyworks Gym for Women (a gym exclusively for women), 53 River St., Cambridge, 576-1493. Classes in weight training, body building, aerobics, belly dancing, yoga, self-defense, and mother/child exercise. Showers, rubdowns, and massage. Open 9:00 a.m. to 9:00 p.m. Mon., Wed., Fri.; 7:00–9:00 p.m. Tues. & Thurs.; 10:00 a.m. to 4:00 p.m. Sat. & Sun.

Body Harmonics, 342 Newbury St., Boston, 536-2225. Emphasis is placed on developing a new set of habits with regard to physical activity through classes in aerobics of various levels and learning the physiology of your body as well as nutrition.

Boston Women's Goju-Ryu, 15 Gertrude Rd., W. Roxbury, 323-3576. Self-defense and karate classes for women, children, and men. Taught by six-time karate champion Pam Glaser.

Back Bay Racquet Club, 162 Columbus Ave., Boston, 262-0660. For a small fee, guests of most major Boston hotels may use the exercise facilities including sessions in fitness, weight training, racquetball, dance, and Nautilus. Mon.–Fri. 6:00–11:30 p.m.; Sat. & Sun. 9:00 a.m. to 9:00 p.m.

The Workout Loft, 91 Newbury St., Boston, 437-7131. Intense

head-to-toe workout including aerobics and exercise to music; shower facilities; classes on a drop-in basis.

Room to Stretch, 105 Newbury St., Boston, 536-0858. Aerobics and exercise classes to music for professional women. Individual consultation as well. No walk-ins; call to reserve a spot, limited class size; 7:30 a.m.–8:30 p.m. Mon.–Fri., 9:00 a.m. to 1:00 p.m. Sat.

Memberships are required for the following clubs:

Women's World Health Spa, 788 Boylston St., Boston, 267-4646; and 200 Massachusetts Ave., Cambridge, 491-3707 and 750 Memorial Drive, Cambridge, 661-3135.

Gloria Stevens Figure Salons, 27 School St., Boston, 523-3098; 194 Alewife Brook Parkway, Cambridge, 492-0805.

Nutri-System Weight Loss Medical Center, 294 Washington St., Boston, Rm. 733-35, 451-6880; 9:00 a.m. to 6:00 p.m. Mon., Wed., Fri.; 9:00 to 5:00 Tues. and Thurs.

Sandy Hagen's Jazz Dance Center, 35 Kingston Rd., Boston, 423-5958. Call for information on their two-hour conditioning class. There are also dance classes in rock-jazz, "luigi"-style lyrical jazz, and tap or ballet.

YWCA of Greater Boston, 140 Clarendon St., Boston, 536-7940. Facilities include a pool, gym, dance studio, and showers. Class times vary; call office 9:00–5:00 for information. Ask about memberships for the Women's Athletic Club.

YWCA of Cambridge, 7 Temple St., Cambridge, 491-6050. Classes in exercise, swimming, aerobics, yoga, karate, and gymnastics. Also a keep-fit program for all ages. Call 9:00–5:00.

*Boston Brahmin Eleanora Sears revolutionized tennis
clothes for women after rolling up her sleeves to play.*

Eleanora Sears, a great-great-granddaughter of Thomas Jefferson, was a pioneer in women's sports, winning over 240 cups for her various activities. Born in Boston in 1881, she made many breakthroughs into previously all-male sports and opened many doors for other women.

Beautiful, rich, outspoken, and independent, she "had the license to do the unconventional," and she often did. Creating an uproar when she arrived at the Burlingame, California, polo field wearing jodhpurs and requesting to be on the team, she was admonished by the Burlingame Mothers' Club and told to "restrict herself to the normal feminine attire in the future."

She played on the Harvard squash courts when women were officially verboten, and revolutionized tennis clothes for women after rolling up her shirt sleeves to play.

She was famous for her long-distance walks and thought nothing of walking from her Beacon Street home to the family summer house in Prides Crossing — a distance of 20 miles. She would sometimes walk the 47 miles from Boston to Providence with her chauffeur and limousine following discreetly behind. She once challenged a few men to accompany her on a walk up the California coast. The men dropped out after 66 miles while she continued without stopping for 108 miles.

She was proficient in fencing, riding, tennis, shooting, squash, baseball, hockey, and polo and even organized a football team on which she played fullback. She drove racing cars and motorboats and was the first Boston woman to fly solo.

Jogging

Most major downtown hotels supply maps to joggers. These maps show safe, well-lighted routes along the Charles River, through the Common and Garden, or through Arnold Arboretum (use in daytime only). The "River Run" is well populated throughout the early morning and early evening. The Paul Dudley White (PDW) path completes a twenty-three to thirty-minute run (3.8 miles) around the lower part of the Charles River.

Racing

Horse: Suffolk Downs, E. Boston, 567-3900.
Harness: Foxboro Raceway, 1-543-5331.
Dog: Wonderland Race Track, 284-1300.

Racquet Sports

For information on public tennis courts in the Boston area, call 725-4006; or for Cambridge, 498-9028. Most courts are on a first-come-first-serve basis, no permit is required, but play time is limited to one hour.

Cambridge Racquetball, 215 First St., Cambridge, 491-8989. You can't reserve a court but they will take you on a walk-in basis on off-hour times. Call for more information.

The Tennis and Racquet Club, 939 Boylston St., Boston, 536-4630. One-time lessons available in court tennis, racquets, and squash. Also weights, whirlpool, sauna, and showers. Open 7:00 a.m. to 11:00 p.m. daily.

Back Bay Racquet Club, 162 Columbus Ave., Boston, 262-0660. For a small fee, guests of most major Boston hotels may play racquet ball and use the exercise facilities.

Roller- and Ice-Skate Rental

Charles River Outdoor Skate Co., 121 Charles St., Boston, 523-9656. Ice-skate and roller-skate rentals as well as skateboards.

Wheels, 270 Newbury St., Boston, 236-1566. Ice- and roller-skate rentals.

Roller- and Ice-Skate Arenas

Skating Club of Boston, 1240 Soldiers Field Rd., Brighton, 782-5900. Tuesday nights only, adult public ice skating.

MDC Skating Rinks (public), call 727-5250 for schedules and info. Murphy Memorial Rink (indoor), Day Boulevard, So. Boston; skate rental. Simoni Memorial Rink (indoor), Gore & 6th St., Cambridge. Steriti Rink (indoor), Commercial St., No. End; skate rental.

Spin-Off, 145 Ipswich St., Boston, 437-0000. This roller-skating disco is decked out with a running waterfall, video screen, and slide show to top-forty music. Open Wed.–Sun. Call for adults' and children's schedules.

Ski Conditions

Massachusetts, Blue Hills, Milton: 828-5070.

New Hampshire, all areas (also summer and foliage events): 1-800-258-3608.

Vermont, all areas,
    1-802-229-0531.

Ski Rentals

The Outback Shop (cross-country), 10 Mt. Auburn St., Cambridge, 491-4173.

The Ski Market (cross-country and downhill), 860 Commonwealth Ave., Boston, 731-6100.

Wheel Works (cross-country), 2044 Mass. Ave., Cambridge, 876-8200.

Soccer

Boston Women's Soccer League, P.O. Box 306, Harvard Square, Cambridge 02138, 864-8181. Any women can join this, the first women's soccer league in the country. The league runs all year round with women of all ages and ability.

Sports Arenas and Civic Centers

Boston Garden: Boston Bruins Hockey, 227-3200; Boston Celtics Basketball, 523-3030.

Fenway Park, Boston, Boston Red Sox Baseball, 267-2525.

Schafer Stadium, Foxboro, New England Patriots Football, 262-1776.

Whale Watching

Boston Harbor Cruises, 1 Long Wharf, Boston, 227-4320.

Windsurfer Rentals

Europa Windsurf, Porter Square, Cambridge, 497-0309.

Can-Am Sailcraft, 48 Charles St., Cambridge, 661-7702.

The Ski Market, 860 Commonwealth Ave., Boston, 731-6100.

NIGHT LIFE

There are any number of interesting bars around the city catering to a wide variety of tastes. The hotel bars offer everything from a quiet tête-à-tête at the Ritz to a rollicking sing-along at the Lenox. Some of the newer hotels (Bostonian, Westin, etc.) have arranged the seating in their bars so that single guests can easily mingle and chat on a friendly, casual basis.

For the more adventurous who are anxious to go out on the town, there is a diverse selection of entertainment to choose from: dance clubs, women's bars, comedy spots, "booze cruises," and even a "pub crawl" where you can join a group to see and enjoy some of the famous Boston bars.

Faneuil Hall Marketplace is a particularly popular spot with women travelers. Not only is it located near several hotels, but there is so much activity going on here that it's quite safe walking around on your own at night.

Lansdowne Street, where the au courant discos are, is another story, however. Car thefts and muggings are frequent here, so don't go into this neighborhood without a friend.

HOTEL BARS

Back Bay Hilton — Satin Doll Lounge
Dalton & Belvidere Streets　　　　　　　　　　　236-1100

Big band music and dancing. Open 5:00 p.m. to 2:00 a.m., closed Sunday.

The Colonnade Hotel — Zachary's Bar
120 Huntington Avenue   424-7000

Offers jazz entertainment, dancing, and complimentary hors d'oeuvres. Open 4:30 p.m. to 2:00 a.m., closed Sundays.

The Copley Plaza Hotel — The Plaza Bar & Library Bar
138 St. James Avenue   267-5300

The elegant Plaza bar with jazz music is a great meeting place. Open 4:30 p.m. to 2:00 a.m. Monday–Saturday, closed Sundays. The Library Bar looks just like a library, with leather chairs and enormous bookshelves. Its dignified setting makes this a spot to finish up business or conduct your own confidential meeting. Open 5:30–10:30 p.m. Monday–Saturday.

The Lenox Hotel — The Olde London Pub
& Grille & Diamond Jim's
710 Boylston Street   536-5300

The O.L. Pub atmosphere is in the style of sixteenth-century England. Happy hour is 4:00–7:00 Monday–Friday serving complimentary hors d'oeuvres. Open 11:30 a.m.–2:00 a.m. seven days. Diamond Jim's piano keeps the sing-along alive and well in Boston. Happy hour is the same as in the Pub. Open 5:00 p.m. to 1:30 a.m.

Boston Park Plaza — The Captain's Piano Bar
50 Park Plaza   426-2000

The piano entertainment starts at 8:00 p.m. every night; Monday–Friday there is happy hour with complimentary hors d'oeuvres from 5:00 to 7:00 p.m.; and on Friday from 5:00 to 6:00 p.m. free champagne is served to women. Open 11:00 a.m. to 2:00 a.m. Monday–Saturday, and Sunday 5:00 p.m. to 2:00 a.m.

The Ritz-Carlton Hotel — The Ritz Bar & The Ritz Lounge
15 Arlington Street   536-5700

Small intimate bar where many a business meeting has been held. Open Monday–Friday 11:30–1:00 a.m., Saturday 5:00 p.m.–midnight; closed Sundays. The Ritz Lounge is very formal and elegant, serving drinks til 1:00 a.m. seven days a week.

The Boston Marriott Hotel — Rachael's Lounge
Long Wharf, 296 State Street   227-0800

Quite the swinging singles disco with a view of the Boston skyline. Happy hour Sunday and Monday serving "double shot" drinks; Monday–Wednesday happy hour serving shrimp 25 cents each; and Thursday happy hour serving complimentary hors d'oeuvres. Open 11:00 a.m. to 2:00 a.m. seven days a week.

57 Park Plaza Hotel — The 57 Lounge
200 Stuart Street   482-1800

Entertainment and dancing with piano and vocals. Open Monday–Thursday 11:30 til 1:00 a.m., Friday and Saturday til 2:00 a.m., Sunday til 11:30 p.m.; entertainment starts at 5:00 p.m.

The Sheraton-Boston Hotel — Mass. Bay Seacoast Co.
39 Dalton Street (Prudential Center)   236-2000

Small nautical bar serving drinks and raw bar items. Happy hour Friday and Saturday 5:00–7:00 p.m. Open 11:00 a.m. to 2:00 a.m. seven days a week.

The Westin Hotel — Turner Fisheries Bar and Restaurant
Copley Place, 10 Huntington Avenue   262-9600

Extremely luxurious setting with excellent service and live jazz entertainment nightly. Raw bar specialties served on the half shell. Open 11:00 a.m. to 2:00 a.m. every day; music plays til 2:00 a.m.

The Hotel Meridien — The Bar at Julien's & Cafe Fleuri
250 Franklin Street   451-1900

The Bar at Julien's has plush sofas, mahogany bar, and piano music. Open Monday–Friday 2:30 p.m. to 1:00 a.m.; Saturday 4:00 p.m. to 1:00 a.m.; Sunday 2:30 p.m. to 1:00 a.m. Cafe Fleuri, a six-story atrium, is open for happy hour only from 4:00 to 7:00 p.m. Monday–Friday, and on Saturday from 8:00 p.m. to midnight has a live band and dancing.

The Parker House — The Last Hurrah & The Parker's Bar
60 School Street   227-8600

The Last Hurrah swings with the popular Winiker Swing Orchestra. There is dancing as well. Happy hour is Monday–Friday 4:30–6:30, with two drinks for the price of one; and complimentary hors d'oeuvres are served from 5:00 to 7:00 p.m. Open Monday–Thursday 11:30 a.m. to 1:00 a.m., Friday and Saturday til 2:00 a.m., and Sunday for brunch. The Parker's Bar has a more relaxed atmosphere with piano music. Open seven days a week: Monday–Friday 11:00 a.m. to 1:30 a.m., Saturday 4:00 p.m. to 1:30 a.m., and Sunday noon to 1:30 a.m.

The Bostonian — Atrium Cafe
Faneuil Hall Marketplace   523-3600

This is one of the most active hotel-lobby bars. Fluffy sofas, picture windows and piano music enhance the atmosphere. Open Monday–Saturday noon to 1:00 a.m., Sunday til midnight; piano entertainment every night.

Hotel Sonesta — Haypenny Lounge
5 Cambridge Parkway, Cambridge   491-3600

Quiet and semiformal; harp music in a subdued atmosphere. Open 11:30 a.m. to midnight seven days a week.

The Hyatt Regency Cambridge — The Pallysadoe & The Spinnaker Lounge
575 Memorial Drive, Cambridge   492-1234

The Pallysadoe resembles a park with its abundant foliage and has entertainment six nights a week with complimentary hors d'oeuvres served from 5:00 to 8:00 p.m. Monday–Friday. Open Monday–Thursday 11:00 a.m. to 1:00 a.m., Friday and Saturday til 2:00 a.m., Sunday noon to 1:00 a.m. The Spinnaker Lounge revolves to give you a constantly changing view of Boston and Cambridge. Open Monday–Thursday 11:00 a.m. to 1:00 a.m., Friday and Saturday til 2:00 a.m., and Sunday noon to 1:00 a.m.

Logan Airport Hilton — The Down One Saloon
Across from Logan International Airport
E. Boston   569-9300

Embellished with mementos of Boston's past, the Down One Saloon offers live music and dancing; and on Friday night, the talent show attracts a lively crowd. Open 11:30 a.m. to 2:00 a.m., seven days a week; entertainment Monday–Saturday.

The Inn at Children's — The Cafe at Sterling's
342 Longwood Avenue   731-4700

Lack of any other good night spots in this area makes the Cafe a popular place. They have a DJ, dancing, and a happy hour Monday–Friday with reduced drink prices and free popcorn. Open 11:00 a.m. to legal closing.

QUINCY MARKET BARS

Cityside
Quincy Market   742-7390

Downstairs at Cityside they feature live entertainment and a happy hour with reduced drink prices and complimentary hors d'ouevres. It's so popular that you can expect standing room only, however. Happy hours 4:00–7:00 Monday–Friday; bar open 11:30 a.m. to 1 a.m. daily.

Guadalaharry's
20 Plimpton Street
(Behind North Market)   720-1190

The first thing you'll want to do here is plant yourself down on one of the overstuffed couches or chairs, then order a margarita served by the glass or mega-liter. There's always lots of activity going on at Guadalaharry's; it's a place to meet people. There are two happy hours: from 4:00 to 7:00 with half-priced drinks, and late-weeknight happy hour from 11:00 p.m. to 1:00 a.m. Bar open 11:30–1:00 a.m.

Houlihans
Quincy Market area,
60 State Street   367-6377

Houlihans is the type of bar where the majority of people stand around and mingle. There's always quite a crowd because this is one of the few bars in the area that has dancing. DJs get the place swinging with top-forty music. Open noon to 2:00 a.m. seven days a week. Happy hour Monday–Friday 4:00–6:30; two drinks for the price of one, complimentary hors d'oeuvres.

Lily's
                                                     227-4242 nights
Quincy Market   227-3434 days

Lily's is known for its piano bar; it has practically become a landmark where on any given night you might hear one of the locals singing along. Bar open seven days a week from 11:30 til legal closing.

Seaside
South Market   742-8728

Amid lots of brass and wood, vast windows, and hanging plants, Seaside bustles with activity. The bar is usually three people deep and the servers are pushed to the max. Complimentary appetizers are served in the lounge all night and drinks are served at the outdoor cafe. No jeans allowed in bar. Bar 11:30–1:00 a.m.

Bunch of Grapes, Landmark Inn
North Market   227-9660

Not to be missed is this sophisticated lounge where vintage wines and champagne are served by the glass with complimentary cheese-and-fruit plate. This is where you can linger in a wing-backed chair, sip a cocktail overlooking the marketplace, and feel as though you've just discovered a secret peaceful hideaway. Bar open until 2:00 a.m.

Lord Bunbury
Faneuil Hall, North Market   227-7004

The setting is typical English-pub-style decor; happy hour is from 4:30–6:30 Monday–Friday. Lively recorded music keeps an upbeat atmosphere. They stop serving food at 4:00 when Bunburys becomes a bar upstairs and down. Open 11:30 a.m. to 2:00 a.m. seven days a week.

LANSDOWNE STREET BARS

Metro
15 Lansdowne Street   262-2424

Voted number-one dance club by *Boston Magazine*. Strobe lights and TV videos augment an already energetic milieu. Dress code calls for no sneakers, t-shirts, or messy jeans or cords. Mostly DJ and recorded music, but some concerts. Call ahead for information. Casual young crowd. Open Wednesday–Saturday, 9:00 p.m. to 2:00 a.m. (Wednesday and Thursday $3 cover; Friday and Saturday $5 cover.)

Nine Lansdowne Street
9 Lansdowne Street   536-0206

Enter through a garage into an enormous warehouse disco with exposed lighting on the ceiling, city skyline reflected on the wall, and balloons in every corner. Laser light show, bubble machines, and snow blowers create an imaginative dancing arena. Open 9:00 p.m. to 2:00 a.m. Tuesday–Saturday (Thursday–Saturday $5 cover; Wednesday $3 cover.)

Spit

13 Lansdowne Street   262-2437

Here the sound is new wave, punk, rock, and reggae. There is no dress code; just "creative dress" or come as you are and then some. Live (local, national, and international) bands are as interesting to see as the people who go to this club. Open Wednesday–Saturday 10:00 p.m. to 2:00 a.m. (Wednesday and Thursday $3 cover; Friday and Saturday $5 cover.)

SOMETHING SPECIAL

Somewhere Else

295 Franklin Street   423-7730

Somewhere Else is the only "women only" bar in Boston complete with an all-female staff. They serve drinks and food; musicians perform and artists exhibit their work. There is no dress code and their security guards will walk you to your car at night. Call ahead for information on special events.

Twelve

1270 Boylston Street   437-1257

Twelve is the largest gay entertainment spot in Boston. There is a piano lounge in the basement, dancing on the first and second floors, and an open-air roof with music on the top floor. A light food menu is served; there are full bar facilities; happy hour is from 4:00 to 9:00 p.m. every day with reduced drink prices; and on Sunday, Tuesday, and Thursday you can get two drinks for the price of one. Open Monday–Friday 4:00 p.m. to 2:00 a.m., Saturday and Sunday noon to 2:00 a.m.

Bull & Finch Pub

84 Beacon Street   227-9605

Located downstairs at the Hampshire House on Beacon Hill, this pub was the inspiration for the TV sitcom, "Cheers." You'll see the front of the pub at the opening of each show. The atmosphere is old-English-pub style with wood beams and bar, authentic red leather seats, and Tiffany-style lamps. Food and drinks are served. Open 11:30 a.m. to 2:00 a.m. Monday–Friday; noon to 2:00 a.m. Saturday and Sunday.

Scotch & Sirloin
77 No. Washington Street   723-3677

One of the reasons we like this place so much is because it's so much fun to get to. Enter the old warehouse (under the red flag), take an elevator up to the second floor, and down the hall is the entrance to this congenial and lively restaurant and lounge overlooking Boston's North End. Thursday–Saturday there is a DJ and dancing (cover $2), with Thursday and Friday being oldies nights; and there's a live band on Wednesday (cover $3). Open 4:30 p.m. to 2:00 a.m. seven nights a week.

Boston Barleyhoppers
c/o Eddie Doyle   227-9605

Boston's only drinking/running club. Their motto is "we run for fun and roam for foam." They've been written up in national publications and in newspapers from Australia to Thailand. You don't have to be a member to join this lively group of enthusiasts who meet at the Bull & Finch Pub at 7:00 p.m. every Monday night and run to other bars around Boston returning back to the Bull & Finch Pub. Call Eddie in the afternoon for more information. (Member fee $5, other $6.)

The Littlest Bar
47 Province Street   523-9766

This little bar is a favorite with local professionals and residents. Typically a neighborhood bar, The Littlest Bar is a fun "sightsee" or a place to have a congenial drink amongst the regulars. Because it's so small (the ventilation is not much to speak of) and closes fairly early, don't plan on staying all night. The phone booth is also the bathroom, which is also the broom closet. 8:00 a.m.–9:00 p.m. Mon.–Sat., closed Sunday.

Three Cheers
290 Congress Street   423-6166

OK now, everyone always says that they have the "best Bloody Mary in town," but what place do you know that doesn't allow the bartender to make them? The chef here fusses over this mixture like a fine soup. It's called "The Bloody Great" or (when ordered without vodka) "A

Bloody Shame." Three Cheers also happens to be a wonderful restaurant and two-story lounge with dancing and roaming a cappella singers. Solid blond oak stairway and bar, brass fixtures, and Victorian furniture. Open 11:00 a.m. to 2:00 a.m. seven days a week; music 9:00 p.m. to 1:30 a.m. Wednesday–Saturday and 1:00–5:00 p.m. on Sunday.

The Boston Pub Crawl
Hub Bus Lines, Inc.   739-0100

Every Wednesday night the famous red double-decker buses make continuous rounds among the best bars and pubs of Boston. For a $2 fee you will visit such famous watering holes as Copley's and the Bull & Finch Pub of TV's "Cheers" fame.

COMEDY CLUBS

The Comedy Connection
Backstage at the Charles Playhouse
76 Warrenton Street, Boston   628-6933

(Located directly behind the Shubert Theatre). Shows Tuesday–Sunday at 9:00 p.m., with a late show Friday and Saturday at 11:15 p.m. Cover $3–5, reservations suggested, closed Monday; presently has forty-five stand-up comedians with shows changing nightly.

Improv Boston
At Satch's Restaurant and Lounge
43 Stanhope Street, Boston
(around the corner from Jason's)   266-2929

Currently running only on Tuesday nights at 8:30–11:00 p.m. (call for possible other evenings). Improvisational comedy with audience participation. Cover $3.

Sam's Comedy Cellar, Play It Again Sam's
1314 Commonwealth Avenue
Brighton   232-4242

Shows Thursday at 9:00 p.m., Friday and Saturday at 9:00 & 11:30 p.m., Thursday $3, Friday and Saturday $4. Call after Wednesday to find out list of "comedy all-stars."

Nick's Comedy Stop
Upstairs at Nick's Restaurant
100 Warrenton Street
Boston   482-0930

Shows are on Friday and Saturday at 8:30 and 11:00 p.m. for $5. Dinner/show package available at $12 (includes a choice of four entrees). Call for possible updated information.

Comedy at Half Shell
Downstairs at the Half Shell Restaurant,
745 Boylston Street, Boston   423-5555

(Across the street from the Prudential Center). Wednesday night at 10:00 p.m. $2–3, Saturday night at 10:00 p.m. $5.

Stitches Comedy Club
969 Commonwealth Avenue   254-3939
Boston   (more information at 254-2054)

Two shows on Friday and Saturday nights at 8:00 p.m. and 11:00 p.m.; Sunday night is open mike at 9:00 p.m. Birthday special: free admissions and a free bottle of champagne on your birthday for you and your friend.

BOOZE CRUISES

Mass. Bay Line Inc.
344 Atlantic Avenue, Rowes Wharf   542-8000

Booze cruises with live entertainment and dancing as well as dinner/dance boats. Call for times and dates.

Boston Harbor Cruises
66 Long Wharf   227-4320

Cocktail cruises with music and dancing. Call for times and dates.

Water Music, Inc.
12 Arrow Street
Cambridge   876-8742

Cruises include the Jazzboat, Cabaret Jazz, Fireworks Specials, and concert cruises. Food and drinks are served on most trips. Call for times and dates.

Best Tours, Inc.
11 Beacon Street   742-4265

Seasonal entertainment, dancing, and moonlight cruises. Call ahead for times and dates.

SHOPPING

ʄʄʄʄʄʄ

SHOPPING ON BEACON HILL

Beacon Hill, with its red-brick row houses, purple-paned windows, gaslights, and brick sidewalks, is the oldest residential part of the city. And the people who live and work here cling tenaciously to their traditions. In 1947, for example, when cobblestone streets originally laid down to provide traction for horse-drawn carts and carriages were first threatened with extinction, a group of indignant neighborhood women protected them from the bulldozer by sitting in the middle of West Cedar Street on the scheduled day of demolition.

As you will see, many of the bricks and even some cobblestones still remain in place. They add greatly to the charm of the hill — but be sure to wear your flat shoes for shopping or exploring here. Many of the steep streets do have iron hand rails, however.

ANTIQUES

Charles Street is the main thoroughfare of Beacon Hill, running from Beacon Street past the Public Garden and through to Cambridge Street at the Longfellow Bridge. As one of the oldest parts of the city, it's fitting that the best antique shopping in Boston can be done here. Amid the flower shops, cafes, and boutiques you will find over two dozen antique shops — from the esoteric Choreo Graphics shop (which specializes in collector's books on dance) to the very British James Billings shop (where you can purchase a George II cabinet for well over $3,000).

Since the turn of the century, Charles Street has been the focal point for antique dealers and traders in Boston. The following pages list some of the outstanding shops with brief descriptions of their specialties. Most of them are open every day (a few closed on Mondays) from 10:00 a.m. to 5:00 p.m. (or, as one dealer said, "until I get bored"); so it's best to call ahead. Many of the shops are also opened on Sunday from 1:00 p.m. until 5:00 p.m.

Albert-Langdon, Inc.
126 Charles St.   523-5954

Oriental antiques, porcelain, paintings, and furniture.

Beacon Hill Thrift Shop
15 Charles St.   742-2323

For over twenty-five years volunteers have been operating this shop — several small rooms filled with antiques, collectibles, and clothes — to raise scholarship money for the New England Baptist Hospital School of Nursing.

James Billings
70 Charles St.   367-9533

Member of the British Antique Dealers Association; fine English antiques and paintings.

Bluefingers
101 Charles St.   523-8774

Vintage clothing, specializing in Japanese kimonos, "funky" 1950s clothes, German army pants, and feather and marabou boas.

Boston Antique Co-op
119 Charles St.   227-9810 or 227-9811

Two levels of fourteen dealers' antiques; a diverse collection from the seventeenth century to art deco — memorabilia, posters, prints.

Butleigh Gate
    82 Charles St.   720-0010

   English and American antiques, furniture, paintings, china, glass, decoys, and Oriental rugs.

Charles Street Trading Post
    99 Charles St. (basement)   367-9551

   Specializes in Victorian furniture, collectibles, and old advertising.

Choreo Graphics
    89 Charles St.   227-4780

   Outstanding collection of books on dance (ballet, folk, modern, ethnic) as well as old books on other subjects.

Evelyn J. Antiques
    118 Charles St.   367-1071

   Vintage clothing, specializing in antique wedding gowns, hats and veils, as well as period dresses made to order.

Eugene Galleries
    76 Charles St.   227-3062

   Antique and rare prints, paintings, maps and books; custom framing.

George Gravert Antiques
    122 Charles St.   227-1593

   Fine antique furniture, art objects, lamps, china, glass, and tapestries.

A. C. Kim
    107 Charles St.   367-1200

   Oriental antiques, furniture, porcelain, and painting, Fuchi dating from fourteenth century.

Samuel L. Lowe, Jr. Antiques, Inc.
    80 Charles St.   742-0845

   Marine antiques — paintings, prints, books, ship models, scrimshaw, and whaling gear.

Marika's Antiques, Inc.
130 Charles St.   523-4520

Oldest shop on Charles St., with diverse collection of furniture, paintings, china, glass, and jewelry.

The March Hare
70 Charles St.   720-4687

Newest shop on Charles St., with English and country antique furniture, collectibles, and accessories.

Pentimento
104 Charles St.   367-4762

The window display indicates haute couture, and while it has some contemporary clothes, it's mostly vintage clothing and collectibles.

Tom Renn
106 Charles St.   247-0800

General antique furniture, paintings, lamps, and decorative accessories.

Shells of England
84 Chestnut St. (just around the corner
from Charles St.)   523-0373

Fine antiques, including period furniture, Orientals, china, porcelain, silver, original prints, and oil paintings.

Sher-Morr Antiques
89 Charles St.   227-4780

General antiques, Oriental art, prints, and collectibles.

The Pig & Saddle
115 Charles St.   227-6113

Oriental and general antique furniture, mirrors, clocks, and paintings.

Times Change
103 Charles St.   227-1668

Specializing in bedroom and closet accessories, armoires, lace pillows, old linens, and handmade quilts.

Weiner's Antique Shop
22 Beacon St. (across from the State
House at Park St.)   227-2894

Since 1896 this shop has specialized in fine American, English, and continental period furniture and decorative arts.

SPECIAL SPECIALTY SHOPS

Besides antiques there are many boutiques and specialty shops along Charles Street with friendly, hospitable proprietors who actually seem to enjoy and encourage browsers. They'll even take the time to chat, answer questions, give directions, and introduce you to their cats.

There's Agatha, for instance, named for Agatha Christie because she likes to curl up and sleep in the mystery section at the bookstore. Sitting in a window of one of the antique stores you'll find Rose (as in "second-hand"); and then there's Jolie, who makes the rounds on Charles Street, but actually lives in Louisburg Square — of course.

Here's a brief description of some of the interesting things you'll find here:

Unique, Etc.
121 Charles St.   523-2825

Solid oak and mahogany reproductions of period pieces, copper and brass items, and weather vanes.

Period Furniture Hardware Co., Inc.
123 Charles St.   227-0758

Large collection of copies and reproductions of antique hardware — doorknobs, pulls, hinges, etc.

The Book Exchange
85 Charles St.   523-4960

New and used books, hardcovers and paperbacks, with a good children's section as well as adults'.

Blackstone's of Beacon Hill, Inc.
46 Charles St.   227-4646

Many interesting gift items from around the world as well as American reproductions.

Eric's of Boston Ltd., Inc.
   38 Charles St.   227-6567

   Stationery, cards, contemporary and antique jewelry, toys, and doll-
house miniatures.

Dutch Cottage Candies
   34 Charles St.   227-0447

   For years Miss Lucy had her own quaint little candy shop, but she
recently moved in next to Fishelson Florist. She has been dispensing
her delicious chocolates and sage advice to neighborhood children for
over fifty-five years on the hill. She has a thing about kids eating "junk"
so you can be sure her candy is nothing but the best.

SHOPPING IN THE BACK BAY

NEWBURY STREET FASHIONS

   Boston has never enjoyed much of a reputation for high fashion.
This is the town where the sensible shoes, the understated dress, and
the vintage coat hold sway. This was the last city in the country where
women gave up white gloves and felt hats, and in fact some never did.

   The one fashion designer not only to survive here but to attract a
sizeable clientele as well, Fiandaca, is of course located on Newbury
Street — Boston's Fifth Avenue.

   Fiandaca Couturier is just around the corner from the Ritz, and
surrounding his shop are a number of contenders for second place:
Charles Sumner, Guy Laroche, Hurwitch Bros., Stuart's, Settebello
Elegantia, and Tat Saunders.

   But the charm of Newbury Street shopping is not particularly tied to
the expensive fashion stores. It has more to do with the small classy
boutiques, the outdoor cafes, and the profusion of art galleries that oc-
cupy once staid old Boston Brahmin town houses.

   You'll find everything here — food, clothing, gifts, accessories —
from the conservative to the super-chic. But Newbury Street is also a
browser's paradise. The decor and uniqueness of the shops is often
more interesting than the merchandise.

   You can easily walk to Newbury Street from most downtown hotels;
but if you plan to drive, be advised that the street's only parking lot
costs about $12 after the first two or three hours. Metered spaces are a
quarter for every fifteen minutes and very hard to come by.

The Bermuda Shop
81 Newbury St.   266-2428

Native Bermudians own this shop. Boston Trader clothes and women's sportswear, and Nantucket lightship baskets.

Bonwit Teller
234 Berkeley Street   267-1200

At the corner of Newbury and Berkeley Streets is the grande dame of all women's clothing stores in Boston, Bonwit Teller. It is housed in a beautiful old building, the former Boston Society of Natural History, and has been the backdrop for countless movies, commercials, and fashion layouts. The clothing is by top designers and expensive, but the sportswear and lingerie, for the most part, are classic and affordable. They also have their own parking lot!

The Cambridge Body Works II
184 Newbury St.   497-0430

Active clothing in natural fibers. Great leotards, hosiery, and shoes. Colorful high-fashion clothing at moderate prices.

Carriage Square
39 Newbury St.   262-7800

Maternity clothing (some imported) and fashions for children in sizes from newborn to toddler. Also wonderful stuffed animals and mobiles.

Chrysalis
154 Newbury St.   353-1166

Clothing for the businesswomen, silk suits, sizes up to 18 + , and one-of-a-kind jewelry including Naga Trade beads. Live models in the windows, on occasion, are real attention getters.

Cuoio
115 Newbury St.   262-0503

Cuoio-designed shoes from Italy. Small collection of designer clothing.

Edward F. Kakas & Sons
93 Newbury St.   536-1858

Furrier. Expensive, of course, but an experience to see. The store resembles a wildlife museum with its life-size stuffed animals seemingly roaming the room.

El Paso
154 Newbury St.   536-2120

Everything in the shop is authentically Western: boots, cowgirl hats, leather moccasins, and clothes.

Freed of London
142 Newbury St.   267-0778

Specializing in exercise gear: cotton leotards, tights, dancewear, and world-famous pointe shoes. This is also a great place to find information on dance and exercise classes around Boston.

Florendena
259 Newbury St.   536-7766

New and used clothing: shoes, coats, suits, and hats. Also a small selection of natural cosmetics.

Forever Flamingo
285 Newbury St.   267-2547

Here the sound is big-band music to go with thirties, forties and fifties furnishings, clothes, jewels, and objets d'art from that era.

Gazelle
118 Newbury St.   267-3215

Some of the finest (and most expensive) high-fashion clothing is here; you can even find one-of-a-kind jogging wear.

Good Times
228 Newbury St.   536-2365

Men's and women's fashions. Great selection of jeans and pants including the Closed name brand.

Goods
130 Newbury St.   536-9770

Specialty lingerie, perfume, potpourri.

Hakikat
110 Newbury St.   266-8548

Indian designer clothing and shoes.

High Society
252 Newbury St.   266-4774

Vintage formal wear including tux rentals, old wedding dresses, and new designer clothing with a touch of yesteryear.

High Society
273 Newbury St.   266-8957

Shop to the sounds of the Beach Boys and other sixties LPs. New and used clothing at good prices — some new-wave gear.

Hope Chest
108 Newbury St.   266-0990

A trousseau shop specializing in silk, satin, and fine cotton lingerie.

Ital
251 Newbury St.   247-3299

Fine footwear for men and women directly imported from Italy. Ital is an exclusive brand.

Italia 2000
125 Newbury St.   266-2984

Designer clothing from Italy.

Javian
156 Newbury St.   536-7516

Classic contemporary clothing for women: weekend and career wear, dresses, and suits. Private label, Denise Hajjar for Javian, exclusively carried at Javian.

J. M. Cook
  139 Newbury St.   266-0885

Wonderful little boutique. Among other things, you can find designer silk pajamas.

Joseph A. Banks Clothiers
  122 Newbury St.   536-5050

Conservative clothing for men and women. Fashionable tailored suits.

Joseph Antell
  140 Newbury St. (2nd floor)   266-6527

Elegant and conservative shoes, mostly imported.

Knitpickers
  115 Newbury St.   267-5989

Handknit sweaters for men, women, and children. Some woven and crocheted. Over fifty local women contribute their talent to this store.

Laura Ashley
  83 Newbury St.   536-0505

Women's and children's clothing, home furnishings, and fabrics by Laura Ashley. A truly beautiful look, with patterns capturing the romantic and innocent expression of an era gone by.

The Lodge
  109 Newbury St.   236-4267

Great sportswear for the prep: Oxford shirts, sweaters, Docksiders. Reasonable prices.

Madison Ave.
  247 Newbury St.   266-4020

Fashions emphasizing casual elegance for the working woman. Moderate prices.

Rae Brewer, Boston
  167 Newbury St.   267-5084

Fine tailored suits, sportswear, and accessories for women.

Riccardi
  128 Newbury St.   266-3158

Expensive haute couture. Jeans with leather laces and other twists.

Serenella
134 Newbury St.   262-5568

Women's fashions by European and American designers; tailored and froufrou. Some accessories.

The Shop for Pappagallo
145 Newbury St.   262-3421

One of the best Pappagallo shops you'll find. Fashionable sportswear and dresses for women as well as great accessories: belts, shoes, hats, and bags.

Tempo
142 Newbury St.   266-7006

Inexpensive up-to-date fashions for women. Known for its great sales. Lots of things are on sale for $6 to $12 off and/or 50 percent off.

Vinicio Paoli
31 Newbury St.   266-6537

Florentine leatherwear and accessories.

NEWBURY STREET GIFTS

Alianza
140 Newbury St.   262-2385

Contemporary handcrafts, jewelry, and quilts.

The Artisans
165 Newbury St.   266-6300

Papier-mache trays, beads, toys, stuffed animals, umbrellas, and baskets.

Body Sculpture
127 Newbury St.   262-2200

Brightly colored silicone jewelry cast in real seashells. Expensive but extremely original.

Cooley's
34 Newbury St.   536-3826

One of Boston's oldest and finest shops for china, crystal, and gifts. Brides have been registering here for generations.

Eastern Accent
237 Newbury St.   266-9707

Japanese crystal stemware, china, blankets, and pillows with an Oriental motif.

Jules
180 Newbury St.   247-1714

Ceramic masks, soft sculptures and dolls, crystal, and unique objets d'art.

La Galeria
244 Newbury St.   262-7001

Trinkets and clothing from Mexico, Peru, and Guatemala. Prints, tapestries, and sculptures made by the owner, Marilyn Tamkin.

La Ruche
174 Newbury St.   536-6366

Antiques, silk flowers, faience dishware, early-American decorative objects, and sweet-smelling potpourri.

Newbury Comic II
332 Newbury St.   236-4930

Old and new comics for the collector, plus price guides for each.

Peking Oriental Imports
159 Newbury St.   262-2947

Baskets! Reasonable prices on bamboo shades, Oriental clothes, shoes, mobiles, and trinkets.

F.A.O. Schwarz
40 Newbury St.   266-5101

One of the most famous names in children's toy stores. Toys, games, and hobbies are sold here. This shop is a pleasure for all ages to visit.

Goods
134 Newbury St.   536-3567

Best stocking-stuffer shop in the world, with nostalgic items such as RCA dogs, Gumby & Pokey, Felix the Cat. Also jokes, gifts, and a great selection of cards. Everything from five cents to $100.

Il Grifo
167 Newbury St.   267-9188

Gift boutique where you can find a replica of the Faneuil Hall grasshopper weather vane. Designed in copper and wrought iron, and costs $95.

In Touch
192 Newbury St.   262-7676

Here you can find some really nice, different Boston t-shirts. Good selection of cards and stationery too.

Irresistibles
161 Newbury St.   267-8080

Bright canvas totes and baggage, belts, hairpins, and jewelry, all in brilliant colors. Also a good selection of Esprit active wear and accessories.

Pierre Deux
111 Newbury St.   536-6364

Exquisite fabrics and gifts from France.

Worlds Apart
123 Newbury St.   236-1367

Folk art and clothing from all over the world. Good selection of Mexican glassware.

NEWBURY STREET HOME FURNISHINGS

Basics
172 Newbury St.   266-9190

You'll find so many functional and practical household ideas here — steel shelves, spice racks, clever gadgets, picnic baskets — that you'll want to redecorate and reorganize your kitchen. The upper level features high-tech racks, basics, and bathroom items.

Bath and Closet Boutique
139a Newbury St.   267-6564

Everything for the bathroom. Brass and porcelain fixtures, towels, and unique basins. Even a wooden tub with copper lining.

Kitchen Arts
161 Newbury St.   266-8701

A large selection of cooking utensils, Wusthof and Henckels knives, fresh-ground coffees; frequent demonstrations by Boston female culinary experts.

Placewares
160 Newbury St.   267-5460

High-tech office furniture for the woman executive. Great porch furniture in natural Danish beechwood with striped canvas covers. Good prices on director's chairs and porch umbrellas.

Scandia Down Shop
166 Newbury St.   536-7990

Down comforters and pillows, domestic and imported sheeting. The shop itself is lovely with its brass beds and Colonial relief ceiling.

The Society of Arts & Crafts
175 Newbury St.   266-1810

Founded in 1897, the Society is the oldest nonprofit crafts organization in the country. Contemporary American crafts in all media as well as handmade one-of-a-kind furniture.

Tile Fashions
85 Newbury St., 2nd level   247-2900

Domestic and imported tiles for kitchen and bath. Extremely reasonable prices on some really attractive tiles.

BOYLSTON STREET SPECIALTY SHOPS

The stretch of Boylston Street from Arlington Street (starting at the Public Garden) up to the Prudential Center offers some of the best shopping in Boston. Here you will find high fashion and unique gifts at moderate prices — a sharp contrast to those of Newbury Street's haute couture. Some of the outstanding specialty shops are the following:

Copley Flair
583 Boylston Street   247-3730

Stationery, wrappings, nostalgia and party items, erotic and exotic cards, wonderful Boston gifts.

Ups & Downs
500 Boylston Street   247-3034

High-fashion clothing at moderate prices.

Elkins
474 Boylston Street   267-7845

Galleria of footwear and boutique. (Clothes upstairs.) Dresses that sparkle with baubles, bangles, and beads. Definitely one of a kind.

Bundles
460 Boylston Street   536-4298

Fun clothing: punk, new wave, and right-up-to-date good stuff.

The Limited
452 Boylston Street   247-0129

High fashion at moderate prices for Juniors and up. Shop to the sounds of rock 'n' roll.

Snyder's Army Navy Store
557 Boylston Street   536-2433

Preppie clothes and clothes for the sport. Large collection of canvas bags; army and navy attire.

Hit or Miss
406 Boylston Street   262-3434 or 262-3435

Twenty to fifty percent off brand-name clothes for women. Also located on Franklin and Tremont streets.

Makanna Inc.
416 Boylston Street   536-6238

Boston's oldest trousseau shop — imported linens and exceptionally fine bedclothes — as well as lingerie and negligees.

Shreve, Crump & Low, Inc.
330 Boylston Street   267-9100

Boston's finest jewelry and gift shop. Wonderful fourteen-karat gold Boston charms (e.g. minuteman, bean pot, swan boat, Mayflower, codfish). Exceptionally fine antiques on second floor.

Elio F.
306 Boylston Street   262-0451

One-of-a-kind clothes specially designed in cotton and in leather. Shoes and wild earrings.

Pier 1 Imports
280 Boylston Street   437-1979

Just about anything imported in the houseware line can be found here. Lots of wicker furniture at reasonable prices; India-type clothing.

Malbens
384 Boylston Street   267-1646

Assortment of foreign and domestic cheeses, natural cheeses, fancy fruit baskets delivered anywhere. Deli sandwiches and great salads made to order. Take-out cups of fruit and yogurt; pastries and candies.

Tellos
364 Boylston Street   536-1565

High fashion at moderate prices. Similar in atmosphere to The Limited (see Downtown Crossing).

Louis for Women
470 Boylston Street   965-6100

The finest in women's clothing; conservative and expensive.

Eddie Bauer
510 Boylston Street   262-6700

Just as good as L.L. Bean. Great clothes for the sport or prep.

The Talbots
458 Boylston Street   262-2981

Just as good as Carroll Reed. Great clothes for the preppy woman.

Tannery
400 Boylston Street   267-0899

Great selection of shoes from the moderately priced to the expensive.

Women's Educational and Industrial Union (WEIU) Shop
356 Boylston Street　　　　　　　　　　　　536-5651

For over a century WEIU has been a nonprofit social service organization providing many services to young and old alike. This beautiful shop (restaurant on second floor) sells exceptionally fine handmade items and needlepoint supplies, as well as some rare and unusual antique items.

SHOPPING IN DOWNTOWN CROSSING

Downtown Crossing is one of the busiest and liveliest areas of Boston. Washington Street, the main thoroughfare and long the mecca for family shopping, is where you'll find the headquarters of Boston's two most popular department stores — Filene's and Jordan Marsh.

The corner of Winter and Summer Streets, which intersect with Washington, is the heart of the area. Pedestrian traffic is so heavy that several streets have now been closed off to cars. Police on horseback monitor the chaos, and street musicians lend a carnival flair to it all.

Just below Winter Street, construction of Lafayette Place — a three-level multi-use complex — is near completion. This will add to the scene another 187 stores (Anne Taylor, Laura Ashley, Carroll Reed, Marimekko, etc.), twenty-three restuarants, the International Continental Hotel, and a large parking garage. With the dearth of good restaurants and parking in Downtown Crossing, this is expected to greatly enhance the city's major retail district.

FILENE'S AND JORDAN MARSH

One of the biggest attractions in Downtown Crossing, one that even Lafayette Place will not supplant, is the legendary Filene's Basement. The line forms early on Monday morning to get the pick of advertised sales — a Saks wedding gown, a Neiman-Marcus fur jacket, Gucci luggage — all at drastically reduced prices.

"FBs" buys out many well-known top designer stores and sells the merchandise at 20 to 90 percent below retail value. They also have an automatic markdown policy every twelve days, so it's not unheard of to get a $500 original designer dress for $30 or less.

There are no frills here. Dresses hang haphazardly from moveable pipe racks, shoes are piled high on tables, and the lack of dressing rooms makes for some strange calisthenics going on in the aisles. Customers often try on garments over and under their clothes, hoping to get a peek at themselves in one of the too few mirrors. (FBs now has a ten-day return policy, which has helped tremendously.)

Besides clothes, FBs has a great gift department, gourmet foods, beauty supplies, jewelry, toys, and many other items.

Jordan Marsh also has a large bargain basement; and while it too sells clothes, some of the best bargains to be found here are in their housewares and linens departments.

Both stores can be reached from the subway (the Washington stop on both Red and Orange Lines), so that you can shop all day without going outside — particularly helpful during snowstorms.

SMALLER CLOTHING STORES

Along with the bargain basements, many of the smaller shops throughout Downtown Crossing and its environs also offer some real values. Copies of famous designers' clothes at specialty shops, shoes and handbags at leather-goods stores, jewelry at the Jewelry Building, top designer clothes far below retail in the garment district, and silk blouses in Chinatown are but a few of the great finds.

Some of the women we talked to who work in the financial district, right next to Downtown Crossing, do almost all of their shopping right here, on their lunch hour.

The Limited
431 Washington St.   426-6952

(Also at Faneuil Hall and 452 Boylston St.) Their clothes and accessories are high on quality and fashion and sold at reasonable prices. Their periodic sales and promotions add to the values to be found here. They carry their own brand, but popular designers' labels are also scattered throughout the store — in dresses, suits, sportswear, separates, outerwear. The saleswomen here are attentive and helpful and will offer to assist you in coordinating a wardrobe.

Hit or Miss
91 Franklin St.   338-5075

(Stores also at 75 Tremont St. and 400 Boylston St.) This store features 30–50 percent off designer clothing along with their own line. Women's sportswear, coats, suits, dresses, sweaters, and blouses, all in Junior sizes as well.

Designer Clothing Ltd.
161 Devonshire St.   482-3335

Top quality and designers (Anne Klein, Givenchy, Cardin, Harve Bernard) can be found here in classic styles. This is discounted first-quality merchandise direct from the manufacturer. Vinnie, the tailor, is on the premises and the people who work here are exceptionally nice.

Billy Vigors
74 Summer St.   426-6259

Forgot to pack your jogging shoes? Sweatshirts? Drop into Billy's for the cheapest sportswear and gym clothes in town. This is an official army surplus store but many name brands can be found here as well.

Sizes Unlimited
40 Winter St.   423-5990

"Big is beautiful" and here's the store to prove it. Everything from evening gowns to jogging suits for larger women — sizes 14½–32½, 38–52. Shoes come in extra widths to EEE, and they offer a full line of lingerie and accessories to complete your wardrobe.

SHOES

Because Boston is a walker's town, you'll find shoe stores almost everywhere — even across from the State House. While most of the shops for high-style imported leather shoes are located in the Back Bay area, their counterparts and copies can be found in the downtown side streets. Many fine shoe stores are found on Temple Place — such as Miller, Bootery of Boston, and Capezio, which cater to special feet. Several stores such as Hayat, Edwin Case, Bakers, Chandler's, and Red Cross feature comfortable, stylish shoes at affordable prices and all are door-to-door on Winter Street.

JEWELRY

Most of the fine old reliable jewelry stores are located in the downtown area, where they have been conducting business since the mid-1800s. E. B. Horn & Co., 429 Washington St. (542-3902) was established in 1839. Homer's at 44 Winter Street (482-1973) has been around since 1882; Roger's at 469 Washington Street (542-2013) since 1904; and De Scenza at 387 Washington St. (542-7975) since 1915.

The Boston Jewelers Exchange Building at 333 Washington Street contains several floors of jewelers who will repair, remake, create, or appraise jewels for you, or sell you some new ones at below-retail prices.

GARMENT DISTRICT

This area, located on the edge of Chinatown, is mostly for wholesalers; but there are several shops that are open to retail customers and well worth the trip down to South Cove. The Howard Building at 75 Kneeland is the location for three such stores.

Lizzie's Place
75 Kneeland St.   426-4291

Located for years in the lobby of the Howard Building, Lizzie recently moved up to the tenth floor along with Flair of Boston. She specializes in handbags and traveling bags in all styles and materials.

Flair of Boston
75 Kneeland St.   426-4291

Located on the tenth floor, you'll find a large assortment of the latest in sports clothes at below-retail costs. Copies of designer clothes that sell at a fraction of the price of the originals make this well worth a trip here.

John Barry Ltd.
75 Kneeland St.   426-4291

When it comes to shopping for women's clothes, this is one of Boston's best-kept secrets. It is located on the tenth floor of the Howard Building along with Lizzie's and Flair. Top fashions and designers' labels abound here (Liz Claiborn, Nipon Boutique, Leslie Fay, etc.), and as their buyer Susan Rosenstein says, "all at wonderful prices." She's right. We bought two pairs of Oleg Cassini slacks for $15 a pair. Dresses, coats, suits, and separates are continually on sale.

Boston's Children's Wear
75 Kneeland St.   482-7048

This store is located in the lobby of the Howard Building and carries a wide selection of babies' and children's clothing as well as toys and stuffed animals.

Harrison Textile
31 Harrison Ave.   426-2116

A huge selection of textiles are on display here, from cottons to fun furs, delicate laces to upholstery fabrics. Many Boston bridal gowns originated here. Patterns, thread, and all the trimmings at super prices, and expert advise to go along with it all.

Koplow Trimming
29 Kneeland St.   426-8549

Just about every kind of trimming, lace, button, sequin, bauble, or bead you'd ever need for dressmaking or crafts can be found at Koplow's. It's a costume-designer's paradise!

Berman Leathercraft
145 South St.   426-0870

Top-quality leather and supplies for making garments. Buckles, belts, buttons, tools, and supplies for leathercrafters.

Yarn and Craft Works Outlet Store
313 Congress St.   357-5391

This shop is directly across from the Children's Museum and has a full selection of top-quality yarn, craft accessories, and kits for knitting, crocheting, needlepoint, and embroidery. Knitting yarns from famous makers are anywhere from 10 to 50 percent off the regular price.

House of Hurwitz
569 Washington St.   423-3143

Hurwitz carries a complete line of toys, novelties, dolls, flags, carnival supplies, and favors; they specialize in quantities for civic groups, churches, and PTA functions.

SHOPPING IN CHINATOWN

As you leave Downtown Crossing, heading toward South Station and the garment district, you will quickly find yourself in the midst of Chinatown. Street signs with Chinese characters and pagoda-shaped telephone booths are among the many colorful decorations here.

Although a fairly small area of town, this is the third-largest Chinese settlement in the country. Number 12 Tyler Street is historically revered as the place where the great Chinese leader, Sun Yat-Sen, plotted the revolution.

While many former residents have now moved to other parts of the city and out into the suburbs, this still remains their main shopping place. Exotic canned foods, live poultry, imported noodles, and fresh bean sprouts are a few of the delicacies sold here.

There are a number of hardware and china shops around, selling the proper cooking utensils for preparing an authentic Chinese meal. Several gift stores selling everything from garish trinkets to exquisite porcelain pieces are located along Beech Street and Harrison Avenue.

Man Ho Co.
62A Beach Street

On a recent trip to Chinatown we found and purchased here (for $22) a beautiful hand-embroidered polyester blouse with covered buttons that looked just like the more expensive silk ones. It comes in several colors and launders beautifully — better than silk.

Cathay Corner
60 Beach Street

They carry a large assortment of vases, porcelain bowls and dishes, lamps and brass items, lacquered boxes, chopsticks, cabinets, and many Oriental wall hangings.

Polynesian Gift Shop
38 Harrison Avenue

Interesting bird cages are featured here as well as inlaid clocks, lovely fans, porcelain dishes, and statues.

Asdour
65 Harrison Avenue

This is a small shop that makes handmade shirts for both men and women.

Chinese American Co.
83 Harrison Avenue

More hand-embroidered silk blouses as well as synthetic ones for sale here, plus books on martial arts and a full line of karate supplies.

SHOPPING AT FANEUIL HALL

The Faneuil Hall Marketplace buildings were erected in 1826 by Mayor Josiah Quincy and were considered one of the most impressive large-scale urban developments in the nineteenth century. In 1973, the Rouse Company of Maryland was chosen to redevelop the buildings into a contemporary urban marketplace.

The Quincy Market building, situated in the middle of the three, now houses food concessions catering to every imaginable taste in a variety of restaurants, sidewalk cafes and delicatessens. The South Market building contains retail shops specializing in fashion apparel, home furnishings, accessories and imports, an arcade with a separate group of small shops within the building, as well as restaurants and bars. The North Market building features an assortment of retail shops selling fashion apparel and accessories, a gallery of small specialty shops, and more restaurants.

Along the way you'll notice the Bull Market which is actually a group of merchants and artisans selling their wares from small carts and stands under bright canopies. Here you'll find everything from souvenirs and leather goods to carts full of dipped gold jewelry or piles of herbs.

The marketplace is one of Boston's most exciting attractions. It is always vibrant and full of life. Banners and flags, cobblestone pavements, and glass awnings all add to the colorful atmosphere. With its restaurants, lounges, shops, and finger foods all contained in one place, you'll need at least one day to see it all.

Because there are so many things to see and not enough room to include them all, the following list contains a selection of our favorite spots.

SHOPS

African Designs

523-2463

Gifts from Africa, Asia, and the Americas. Great selection of unique baskets and mobiles, hand-carved animals, tapestries, jewelry, and shuffle shoes from Cathay; very reasonable prices.

Boxes

742-2663

If you're one who loves boxes and small containers, you'll love this attractive little shop. Boxes here are made of tin, straw, wood, paper, ceramic, Dedham pottery, and just about anything else you can think of.

The Bear Necessities

227-2327

This shop is unbearably fun. Teddies in all shapes and sizes, old and new, plus all sorts of bearaphernalia for the collector of, or just lovers of, teddy bears.

Dalliance

367-9192

Exotic lingerie and nightwear. Delicate teddies and gowns in soft, luxurious silks and satins.

Frillz

227-1028

Beautiful one-of-a-kind hand-painted clothing for women and children. Splashes of floral colors and designs enhance simple but fashionable white cottons, sweats, and frills.

Have a Heart

661-3852, ext. 474

Hearts, hearts, and more hearts. Everything in this shop wears a heart or is a heart. The biggest collection you'll ever find in one spot, with prices starting as low as five cents.

Hog Wild

367-9520

Home of the world-famous Pigmania game and the Calvin Swine collection. The word here is "pigs." Stuffed animals, t-shirts, stationery, and jewelry. Drop in and . . . pig out.

Jasmine

742-4759

Women's and Juniors' fashionable sportswear at reasonable prices including a great selection of bags, belts, hosiery, shoes, and gifts.

Le Bon Voyage

523-6640

Everything the traveler could want. Canvas luggage and bags, passport cases, maps, headphone sets, toiletries, and film.

Natural Image

523-5150

Custom-made women's clothing in natural fibers; cotton frilly dresses and hand-knit sweaters.

Over the Rainbow

227-2040

All-natural cosmetics and skin care with the largest selection of colors in Boston. A variety of shades with glitters and highlights, and nothing over $7 in the makeup line. Accessories and gifts are also available.

Pottery Cellar

742-3211

This underground shop boasts the best collection of baskets in the market. They also carry mugs from Japan, Boston baked-bean pots, and New England Bennington pottery.

Sweet Stuff

227-7560

Be forewarned, once inside this store you'll literally be surrounded by candy. From floor to ceiling it's jelly beans et al. And as long as you're there, don't forget to try the gourmet chocolates and homemade fudge.

Whimsey Woolsey

523-5499

Here you'll find sheep galore. Whether they're stuffed animals, trinkets, or sheep-sheared yarns, you'll agree this shop is un-baaa-lievably cute.

QUICK FINDS

Aspirin

Quincy Market: Tobacconist Ltd., 523-8468

Bank

North Market: Shawmut 24, twenty-four-hour automatic cash for Shawmut Way cardholders

Cards/Stationery

North Market: Goods Department Store, 367-9010
South Market: Bassil & McNichols Ltd., 367-1050
Quincy Market: Postop, 227-2334

Cigarettes

Quincy Market: Tobacconist Ltd., 523-8468
Faneuil Hall Wine and Spirits, 742-6539

Film & Camera

North Market: Le Bon Voyage, 523-6640
Quincy Market: Picture You, one-hour developing, 720-2110
Polaroid for Instants, camera loans, 227-4722 and 227-4723

Flowers

North Market: Faneuil Hall Flower Market, 742-3966
Quincy Market: Produce House, will sell single flowers, 742-2545

Keys & Locksmith

North Market: Locks & Keys Inc., keys made while you wait.

Liquor

Quincy Market: Faneuil Hall Wine & Spirits, singles, sixes and
wines, 742-6539

Maps

North Market: Le Von Voyage, 523-6640
Quincy Market: The Cookbook Store, 723-4694
Postop, 227-2334

Monogramming

North Market and Quincy Market: Monograms, 523-5484

Parking

Indoor Parking Garage: Located at the waterfront end of the North
Market building and behind the Lord
Bunbury restaurant. Rates: for three to
nine hours, $8.

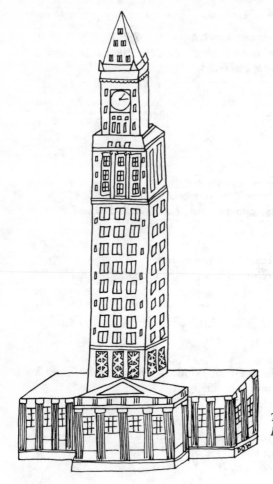

"Like a four-sided wedge
The Custom House Tower
Pokes at the low, flat sky."
(Amy Lowell, poet).

Restrooms

North Market: Next to J.A. Parker and Pappagallo
South Market: Next to Bassil & McNichols Ltd. and This End Up
Quincy Market: Lower level underneath The Magic Pan Restaurant and next to Swensen's Ice Cream

Shopping Bags

North Market: Next to Judie's Fragrances, 723-6256
Quincy Market: Faneuil Hall Wine & Spirits, 742-6539

Stamps & Mailbox

Quincy Market: Postop, 227-2334

Sunglasses

North Market: Sun Vision, 367-3428

Tampons Etc.

Quincy Market: The Tobacconist Ltd. 523-8468

Umbrella

North Market: Le Chapeau, 227-3085

SHOPPING IN THE NORTH END

Boston's "Little Italy" is a world unto itself. Cut off from the downtown area by the John F. Kennedy Expressway, this once fashionable
part of town is now a crowded, bustling tenement and business district.

Noisy kids play ball in the middle of the narrow streets, old women
sit and watch from second and third floor windows, and men congre-
gate along the busy sidewalks swapping stories and arguing in Italian.

Haymarket Square on the Boston side of the Expressway, an integral
part of the North End, is filled on weekends with vendors shouting
their wares. Fruits, vegetables, and fresh cuts of meat and fish are displayed in the open and sold here at below-supermarket prices. Many
city dwellers as well as people from the suburbs do their marketing here
on Friday nights or Saturday afternoons.

There is a pedestrian walkway under the Expressway leading into
Salem and Hanover Streets. Hanover is the main street of the North
End and it is lined with bakeries, restaurants, cafes, and neighborhood
stores. Food is big business here, and some of the best cooking in town
is done right around here — and mostly by women chefs.

The site of the oldest bakery in America is at 99 Salem Street where
the bread for the Continental army was baked. And close by on Fleet
Street was once located the first factory to introduce macaroni to this
country.

This is a great daytime area for browsing, tasting, and smelling; but
other than food, shopping is of little interest here. If you've never had a
crespelle be sure to stop at any one of the bakeries along Salem or Hanover for this treat — fried dough, liberally sprinkled with honey, nuts,
and confectioners' sugar — and forget the calories.

THRIFT SHOPS

Thrift shops have finally come of age, so to speak, and if you've never visited one, Boston is a good place to start. Some of these shops have been around for a long time; indeed, some are now selling to their third or fourth generation of customers. Many of the newer stores feature so-called "vintage" clothing, but all have quality, stylish, clean, used clothing at a fraction of the original price. Other than the ones run by organizations, almost all are exclusively women-owned businesses.

Bargain Box
117 Newbury St., Boston   536-8580

The Junior League of Boston has been running this shop for many years at this prestigious location. Much of the merchandise originated at one or another of the neighboring expensive, fashionable stores along Newbury Street. There's always a good selection here of women's dresses, coats, suits, and sportswear as well as jewelry and gift items.

Beacon Hill Thrift Shop
15 Charles St., Boston   742-2323

This quaint little shop has been operated by volunteers for over twenty-five years to help raise funds for nursing scholarships at the New England Baptist Hospital School of Nursing. There are several rooms filled with clothes, antiques, collectibles, books, and household items that have been donated by loyal supporters. The last time we dropped by there we saw a complete set of Lenox china at a remarkably low price.

The Closet
223 Newbury St., Boston   536-1515

Originally this was for men only, featuring hardly worn hand-me-downs from Louis and Brooks Brothers. It now carries women's clothing as well, with nothing but the best labels and nothing over three years old.

Bluefingers
101 Charles St., Boston   523-8774

This is one of the top vintage-clothing shops around; it features antique Japanese kimonos; styles from the 'forties and 'fifties; feathers; boas; and all that funk, punk, and rock stuff.

Morgie's
(Morgan Memorial Goodwill Industries, Inc.)
95 Berkeley St., Boston   357-9710

A few years ago, Morgie's ripped out all the designer labels from their well-worn jeans and stitched in their own Morgie labels. They became the latest status jeans around and sold like hotcakes. Clothing, small appliances, sports equipment, records, and books are just a few of the offerings here. Handicapped men and women work for Goodwill keeping this merchandise repaired, updated, and cleaned.

Encore Exchange
318 Harvard St., Brookline   566-4544

This is another store that had been in business long before the new wave of thrift shops. Clothes with nothing but designer labels will be found here in tip-top condition — plus mink and sable coats!

Fashion Exchange
144A Harvard St., Brookline   277-4125

A small but neat little shop with great designer fashions at terrific prices; they even have a layaway plan.

R.G.F. Antiques
195 Harvard St., Brookline   734-2226

Vintage clothing with an emphasis on Victorian white wedding dresses, camisoles, petticoats, and pantaloons.

RARE BOOKS

There are many new and used bookstores throughout Boston and Cambridge (particularly the Harvard Square area) but here are a few of the best for old, used, or rare books:

Avenue Victor Hugo
339 Newbury St.
(Mass. Ave.), Boston   266-7746

New and used books and magazines; well organized for a quick back-issue search.

Book Case
   42 Church St. (in Harvard Sq.)
   Cambridge   876-0832

   Large selection of used books. Very good Women's Studies section
— many out of print.

Brattle Book Shop
   9 West St., Boston   542-0210

   Legendary old favorite used-book store; the helpful proprietor,
George Gloss, keeps track of books by Boston women authors.

Glad Day Books
   43 Winter St., Boston   542-0144

   This is a lesbian and gay bookstore with a large selection of lesbian
and feminist books, periodicals, records, and greeting cards.

Goodspeed's Book Shop
   7 Beacon St., 2 Milk St., Boston   523-5970

   Rare and secondhand books, autographs, prints, and expert ap-
praisers.

New Words Bookstore
   186 Hampshire St., Cambridge   876-5310

   A bookstore filled with women's books (past and present), newspapers, magazines, posters, buttons, t-shirts, and a bulletin board covered with the latest information on women's activities in Boston and
Cambridge.

Starr Book Co.
   186 South St., Boston   542-2525

   Another old used-book store that maintains a long list of women's
books and will do a search for out-of-prints.

LAST-MINUTE SHOPPING

   Whether you're taking home a souvenir of Boston for yourself or for
a child at home, or you're in need of a thank-you gift for a hostess or
business associate, here are some suggestions to make the job easier.

Books

The Museum Shop at the Old State House has an excellent collection of books about Boston and New England. One particularly fascinating selection is *The Journal of Madam Knight*, a true and amusing account of a daring journey by Sarah Knight, who took off on her own in 1704 from Boston to New York — an unheard-of thing for a woman to do in those days. *Make Way for Ducklings* by Robert McCloskey has been a children's classic for years and tells about a family of mallard ducks in Boston. Any number of beautifully illustrated books on Boston are available here as well.

Boastfully Boston

Miniature swan boats in ceramic by Sebastian; authentic reproductions of Colonial brass candlesticks or brass doorknockers; hand-carved (to order) reproductions of eagles; Boston Harbor Tea Party set packed and shipped by the same London firm which supplied the tea in 1773 for the original Boston Tea Party; all of the above can be purchased at the Museum Shop at the Old State House.

Rose Medallion ware similar to that which was part of Boston's nineteenth-century China trade is sold in Chinatown at Cathay Corner, 60 Beach Street, and several other shops in this area.

A replica of the Faneuil Hall grasshopper weather vane, designed in copper and wrought iron, can be purchased at Il Grifo, 167 Newbury Street.

Boston t-shirts are sold just about everywhere in town. Some of the nicest ones are at In Touch (192 Newbury Street); at the Kennedy Studios (647 Boylston and several other locations); and in some of the Bull Market carts in Quincy Market.

Flowers

The Ritz-Carlton Flower Shop at 6 Newbury Street will arrange flowers or a plant in various-sized swan boats; Victorian Bouquet Ltd. at 53A Charles Street has an unusual selection of imported flowers and plants; and for the truly exotic, try the florist shop, Plantae, in the lobby of the Westin Hotel.

Scrimshaw/Simshaw

Scrimshaw is the ancient art of carving pictures and designs on whale bone or elephant tusks. New England sailors during the days of the whale fishery whiled away their time at sea by creating jewelry and trinkets for their families back home. Scrimshaw has always been a valued gift. Now however, the needless killing of whales and elephants is outlawed; so modern-day scrimshanders use a synthetic polymer "ivory." Old pieces of authentic scrimshaw can still be found in many local antique shops, and the synthetic "simshaw" is on sale at several gift shops in Quincy Market as well as at the Museum Shop at the Old State House.

Copley Place

One of the most exciting and expensive developments ever to be built in Boston is the spectacularly new Copley Place that recently opened its doors (February 1984). It brings a whole new international flair to Boston shopping.

It is a multilevel, glass-enclosed shopping mall linking the historic Back Bay and the South End and built over the Massachusetts Turnpike. Anchored by the three-story Neiman-Marcus department store, a fabulous gallery of world-famous shops such as Gucci, Yves St. Laurent, Turtle Books of France, and Liberty of London (just to mention a few) fill the elegant corridors.

There is a nine-screen Sack Theatres cinema complex along with a variety of New England style restaurants — including Boston's own Durgin Park. The Commons, a gourmet cafeteria, is already showing signs of becoming the "in" gathering place.

A glass-enclosed walkway from the Westin Hotel provides shoppers with a year-round, climate-controlled area to browse in with over 100 stores and restaurants to choose from. Some of the old-world charm of Boston — bowfront windows, leaded glass, rosewood and brass trimmings — have been incorporated into this space-age marvel.

Even if you don't like to shop, the 80-ton water sculpture made of granite, travertine and marble that dominates the nine-story atrium makes a trip to Copley Place well worthwhile.

INDEX